DRIVING DAISY

By
Pauline Arnold

MAPLE
PUBLISHERS

Driving Daisy

Author: Pauline Arnold

Copyright © 2025 Pauline Arnold

The right of Pauline Arnold to be identified as author of this work has been asserted by the author in accordance with section 77 and 78 of the Copyright, Designs and Patents Act 1988.

First Published in 2025

ISBN 978-1-83538-259-2 (Paperback)
      978-1-83538-260-8 (E-Book)

Book Cover Design and Book Layout by:
    White Magic Studios
    www.whitemagicstudios.co.uk

Published by:
    Maple Publishers
    Fairbourne Drive, Atterbury,
    Milton Keynes,
    MK10 9RG, UK
    www.maplepublishers.com

A CIP catalogue record for this title is available from the British Library.

All rights reserved. No part of this book may be reproduced or translated in any form or by any means, electronic or mechanical, including photocopying, recording or by any information storage and retrieval system without written permission from the author.

The views expressed in this work are solely those of the author and do not necessarily reflect the publisher's opinions, and the publisher, as a result of this, disclaims any responsibility for them.

For my wonderful family and friends.

Foreword

I have been persuaded that I should write about my adventure in Daisy my beautiful old VW Campervan and so here goes.........

Have you ever thought you would like to take off and leave everything behind for a while? Well I did and this is a story about that adventure.

It happened because my husband, Richard died unexpectedly and my world was completely turned upside down.

I know everyone is affected differently by grief and I must have appeared to be coping well but in reality I was struggling. I missed him so much and often woke up in the middle of the night, even two years later, trying to work out if there was anything I could have done to prevent his death. Sometimes I could feel really positive about the future and then on others when the wave of emotion hit like a Tsunami, I felt as though I couldn't go on. However, one morning I woke up with a really strong conviction that I should go travelling in this country and that I should buy an old VW campervan.

My diary for that day is headed 'momentous decision'. It was ridiculous as, firstly, I didn't have the funds to do it and secondly, I absolutely hate driving but this idea kept nagging at me. I know that it is usual for the child to go to the parent for a loan but on this occasion it was a case of role reversal. It just so happened that my son Neil had decided to sell his house in York, planning to invest some of the proceeds into their new house in London and some into his pension fund. I eventually plucked up the courage and asked him if he would like to invest some of the money in a project of mine and I explained the project. I assured him that I would repay the loan with interest at some point and so he shouldn't be financially out of pocket. How typical of Neil, rather than trying to talk me out of going he said yes straight away and loaned me £25,000, adding that he thought it was a brilliant idea. This was crazy, I am a 'stay at home' person who absolutely hates driving and yet here I was at my great age planning some sort of road trip and lo and behold, it seemed to be gaining momentum and something I was totally unable to control.

At this time, I only ever intended it to be 'A bit of an Adventure'. I had no thoughts of undertaking a pilgrimage and in fact I always imagined people who undertook pilgrimages would do so by walking for miles and miles barefoot with the weight of the world on their shoulders, a bit like Christian in The Pilgrim's Progress which I had read as a child. However, whilst in Wales I emailed my friend Lindsay and asked if you had to be on foot to undertake a pilgrimage. She emailed me back with the definition 'a journey to a shrine or sacred place as an act of devotion in order to acquire spiritual merit or as a penance' no mention of 'on foot'. Although I wasn't aware of what I was doing at the time, I reckoned that pretty well fitted with what happened and so this story is about an adventure which became something more!

INDEX

Chapter 1 – Foreword 4

Chapter 2 – Finding Daisy 7

Chapter 3 – Ready to go! The Atlantic Highway 16

Chapter 4 – Gower Peninsular and other places May 17th - June 8th . 34

Chapter 5 – Pembrokeshire and Cardiganshire June 8th – June 18th 53

Chapter 6 – The Llyn Peninsula, Snowdonia and Anglesey
June 18th – June 29th 65

Chapter 7 – An aside 77

Chapter 8 – Chester, Liverpool, The Peak District and
Lancashire June 30th – July 13th 79

Chapter 9 – Cumbria, the Lake district and Northumberland
July 13th – August 1st 91

Chapter 10 – The Lowlands of Scotland August 1st – August 17th ... 110

Chapter 11 – Northumberland and Durham
August 17th – August 27th 129

Chapter 12 – North Yorkshire and North Lincolnshire
28th August - 7th September 142

Chapter 13 – Norfolk and Suffolk 7th - 24th September 157

Chapter 14 – The End of the journey 177

Chapter 15 – Reflections 192

Acknowledgements etc. 204

Chapter 1

Finding Daisy

I started to share my thoughts of the trip with family and friends and rather than them saying 'no don't do it' which was what I was expecting them to say (and maybe deep down hoped that is what they would say) they were on the contrary very supportive and thought it a great idea. Only two days later I was even sharing my idea with Ian who cuts my hair only to find out that he had owned an old split screen VW some years ago, he said they are 'great fun' and of course very sought after these days. He was very encouraging and told me to have a go and undertake an adventure.

By the end of August I had started to plan. My amazing friend, Carol went immediately into support mode and started bringing me magazines about VW campervans. It was at this point I asked myself 'Why an old VW campervan? The answer was that I didn't have a clue why it had to be, only that it seemed to be a part of the plan. The old split screens are beautiful but way out of my price range and so after much research I decided that the VW Devon Bay was a contender. How to go about finding one?

Strangely enough, I came across a company in Cornwall (I live in Cornwall) who rented out old VW Devon Bays for holidays and so I thought I would give them a call to enquire how much it would cost to hire one only to be told they were for sale. The company had recently been taken over and they were concentrating on letting out the new VWs only. This seemed as though it was meant to be (a dangerous thought). At the beginning of November I went to have a look at them, Carol came with me. Trying to find the place was an adventure in itself but after travelling down many terrifyingly narrow and potholed lanes we eventually found the place we were looking for. The couple who owned the vans were delightful and after looking at Maggie May and Delilah's credentials we went to look at the vans. Maggie May was a 1972 Bay and had more recent fittings than Delilah but, of course, it was Delilah that I fell in love with. She was red and white with beautiful retro curtains and fittings. I had a test drive (really scary) so different to a modern vehicle, no power assisted steering, a very different gear change and guess what, the indicators don't go back on their own. I was assured I would soon get used to it, (um! not so sure). I was in a complete emotional turmoil and we got totally lost on the way home.

Carol was brilliant, very supportive as usual and we found it hilarious but I realised that she was probably thinking that I was mad to go for an old VW and if I couldn't even find my way around a part of Cornwall close to home, what chance did I have of navigating myself around the country? Where to go to from here?

It became even more obvious that Carol wasn't as star struck on Delilah as I was, as the day after she started sending me links to more modern and sensible campervans. The trouble was, as ridiculous as it was, I was still hooked on the idea of an old van, so much more romantic.

I really needed someone to have a look at Delilah but after contacting various garages it became obvious that they knew nothing about old VW's and so I went to see Peter who has a garage which specialises in old Land Rovers. He was so helpful and he spent some time chatting to me about old VW's and he agreed to have a look at Delilah for me. It so happened he had to deliver a vehicle back to a customer who lived not far away. He didn't charge me for it, such an act of kindness. However, his verdict wasn't what I was hoping for, he reported that 'she has serious rust issues which have been patched with fibreglass and are now breaking through again, she will need a serious amount of money spent on her soon'. Oh dear! So disappointing as I really thought she was the one. Peter said he would speak to a friend of his to see if he could help.

My search came to a bit of a halt for a while as my beautiful Blue Roan Cocker Spaniel Bertie died. He had been diagnosed with a mouth tumour around six months earlier and he had been deteriorating ever since but I still felt such a tremendous sense of loss when he was finally gone. It was January before I returned to the 'trip'.

I saw Peter again and he had discovered that there was a company on the north coast of Cornwall that specialises in restoring old VW's called Evil Ben's. I 'phoned Evil Ben, an expert on VW's (by the way he isn't at all evil) and explained what I was looking for. He was really helpful and said he would help me to find a van. Everything suddenly seemed possible. He came back almost immediately, his friend had just finished restoring an old VW but wanted £22,000 for it. The £25,000 I had borrowed had to finance the whole trip and so unfortunately it was beyond my budget. He said he would keep looking. I found a van called Lottie on ebay but the asking price was £18,000, Ben suggested I offer £14,000 which wasn't acceptable. I was wasting a lot of time looking at vans on ebay and so gave up on that avenue. I really didn't know what I was looking for, I was just going by whether or not I liked the colour and name.

I was starting to get really desperate as I wanted to leave early April and so I did something really stupid. I emailed to see if Delilah was still for sale. I suppose this feeling that she was the one hadn't totally left me. She was still for sale (that should have told me something but oh no! I blindly went on) and so I went to see her again, this time as I thought without my rose-tinted glasses on. I still liked her but had to admit she was pretty rusty although I still loved her interior. Took photos and showed them to Ben. Her asking price was £16,000 but he said she was definitely worth no more than £12,000. My offer of £13,000 was accepted. Oh dear, what had I done! I contacted Ben to see if he could do the work on her but when he went and saw her for real, he strongly recommended that I withdraw the offer! This threw me into a right quandary as I believe that your word is your bond and all that. As I mentioned, the couple who owned Delilah are lovely and when I explained they graciously let me withdraw. I still felt really bad as I had put an awful lot of people to an awful lot of trouble.

January went by and then February, still no van!

Early March I spotted Geraldine was for sale locally. I had passed this van on a number of occasions, you couldn't miss it as it was covered in CND and other psychedelic images. It occurred to me at this point that maybe I was trying to go back to my 'Hippy' days. I contacted Ben. Fortunately, he knew her and advised she was very rusty under a vinyl coating. Not good news. However, only days later Ben 'phoned to say that he had a van in for me to see. Whoopee!

I think Ben will forgive me for saying that his garage is like no other. It is situated on a small industrial estate and to get to it you pass other companies on a potholed road. It had rained heavily the day prior to going to find him and so the pot holes were full of water. Evil Ben's is situated at the very end, overlooking a lovely valley. As you would expect to find, there are the mechanical repair areas like any other garage and a paint body spraying shop. However, outside you will see an array of old VW's of all sorts of shapes and sizes from the original VW Beetles to the customised VW Bays and some weird and wonderful contraptions that I have never seen before and all in a state of needing a lot of TLC. Some of the customised VW vans are quite a work of art with lowered bodies, individually designed and hand painted, incredible interiors which include skulls and other artefacts that their proud owners wished to adorn them with. I'm sure they are very different from when they came off the production line. I digress. The van I have come to see is a 1979 Westfalia. My first reaction to this van was that it was very 'orange'. This is a bit unfair as actually she is more of a mustard colour and has a white top, she had no name then, plus it felt very 'male'. Her interior was certainly retro but not what I had envisaged. Added to everything else she was a left-hand drive. If I'm honest, my heart sank, it certainly wasn't love at first sight.

I must have expressed all this out loud as Ben and his colleagues came up with suggestions for what could be done. If I was going on this trip this year, I didn't have a choice as time was running out and they assured me that there would be no problem with it being left-hand drive. Ben negotiated the deal for me and Daisy was mine. Phew, phew, phew. What had I done?

This was the most enormous leap of faith as I didn't even drive her, I just sat next to Ben who muttered that this and that needed a tweak and he wasn't entirely happy with the way the gears were working etc.etc.etc. I left the van with Ben to be sorted out.

There were numerous phone calls between us over the coming weeks and I decided I needed some modifications to be done; it was discovered that the gas heater was dangerous and had to come out and it didn't have a fridge and so space had to be found for an electric cool box. I haven't even mentioned any of the mechanical issues. However, I eventually had a working van at a reasonable price.

I still hadn't plucked up the courage to drive the van and so asked Ben if he could deliver it to my home. Ben drove it on to the drive on the 13 April at 6.15pm. Again, I thought what have I done? I didn't even know if I could drive her! A large gin and tonic was called for, as I started to panic.

I have to say I must have been a right thorn in Ben's side over those months but he and his lovely wife only ever showed kindness and the guys who worked for him always seemed gentle souls with their alternative surfing lifestyles and dreadlocks, so helpful on my many visits.

As mentioned, I had been over to see the van whilst it was being worked on and the colour was gradually growing on me but it had to have a name. The day after it arrived, Jon, Carol's husband, came over to see it. He has a beautiful blue and cream very early Land Rover and so is used to driving old vehicles and was empathetic with me over wanting an old vehicle. There were a few fixings missing inside the van and so he returned later after searching through his 'come in handy box' with various bits and pieces to sort it out. When Ben delivered the van he just drove it through the fairly narrow gateway and left it at the bottom of my drive which isn't an easy drive to negotiate even in a car as it is quite narrow, turns and is on a hill. Jon obviously realised that I would have difficulty backing out onto the lane and so very kindly offered to turn it around for me so that I could go out frontwards. I honestly believe that if he hadn't done that it would be sat there now and I wouldn't have gone anywhere.

At 6.30am that Sunday morning (I had figured there would be less vehicles on the road at that time) I turned on the ignition. I had to give myself a 'good talking to', my heart was pounding, my stomach churning but it had to be done. It is fair to say that I set off in a state of fear and trepidation, so different to driving a new vehicle, so much more thinking time needed before actually approaching a junction. However, I followed a carefully planned route without incident. In fact, on my way home I came back on a narrow lane and saw a friend, I passed her and waved furiously, 'I don't dare stop' but I could see the look of surprise on her face. When I got back I had hoped to reverse her in backwards but just typical, there was a car up behind me and so I had to go in frontwards, she was pointing in the wrong direction again. However, I could do it, I could drive her! The left-hand position was fine, I just had to remember to stay close to the kerb.

My sense of elation was deflated the following day. I went to start her and nothing. The starter motor was turning over but nothing was happening. I had to call for help. I was very fortunate in that the guy who came to see her knew about VW's and it wasn't long before he had diagnosed 'no petrol' (I guess you don't need to be a rocket scientist to figure it out but I hadn't even considered this). The petrol gauge wasn't working.

Whilst waiting for Daisy to be sorted I had sourced all manner of essential and, of course, 'non-essential but can't do without' items. One of those items, an extremely luxurious 'Dusk' mattress topper. It has two parts filled with feather and down. The seats pull out to form a pretty comfortable bed and so this was just the icing on the cake. As well as cooking items I had bought - a super retro bright green kettle, retro bowl and tray etc. plus champagne glasses (you never knew if they might be needed).

The maiden Voyage! It was a glorious day with blue skies and scudding white clouds. Perfect! I had agreed to meet up with my friends Ann and Pete at a camping site on the north coast of Cornwall situated on the cliff tops overlooking Watergate Bay. They had offered to show me the ropes as they have had a very sensible modern campervan for some time. It was a brilliant couple of days although not without incident. On the way I had agreed to take the van back to Evil Ben's as the sliding door wasn't working properly and somehow managed to get lost and ended up on a housing estate (this was the first but not last time this would happen). I had to do a three-point-turn which ended up being at least eleven points (I just hoped no one was watching), but my navigation eventually was successful and I found the site which was in a stunning location and even more importantly, I found Ann and Pete. After the booking-in procedure, they showed me how to do the electric hook-up etc. I could relax. I had a certain sense of elation at this point as here we were, sat around on a fabulous afternoon drinking tea, with the sea just a stone's throw away catching up with the news and gossip, Daisy all hooked up and looking beautiful, somehow I had done it.

Early evening whilst the sun was still warm we walked down to the beach and walked along the sand to the hotel where Pete treated us to an amazing meal. Much later feeling rather full and very mellow from the wine, we walked back to the site accompanied by a fantastic setting sun over the water, so beautiful. A starry night followed and so bolstered by wine and one of Ann's very generous night caps I spent my first night in Daisy. She was so comfortable and I had no trouble going to sleep under the starry sky. For the first time in ages I slept like a log, it was so peaceful. I joined Ann and Pete for breakfast and then it was time to drive home. It had been a lovely couple of days and I now felt confident with the process of finding and booking-in to the sites. Daisy had behaved like a dream, very comfortable for one person. The bucket system proved to work well (just in case of emergencies) as did most other things but it was no good, I would have to get the fuel gauge sorted.

Back Daisy went to Evil Ben's. Neil had come down to spend a few days with me and so we went in convoy and left her there.

Furious activity took place over the next few weeks. More bits and pieces were needed for the trip, the house had to be sorted, the garden to be left in some sort of order. Jo and the family were coming to live in the house and so I had to store a lot of my 'stuff' in the attic and summerhouse.

It was on one of my early morning walks with Carol that we eventually decided on Daisy for her name. Buttercup, Annabelle, and many others had been contenders but somehow Daisy seemed to suit. As a plus it was fairly easy to get van stickers for that name; it had to be done. Suddenly she was adorned with daisies although I tried to be fairly restrained. It was weird but now all my early fears about her had disappeared and she felt right.

Friends had started to buy me VW memorabilia, tea caddy, mini VW's, all sorts of things plus Ann sent me the VW bible. I had made an awning for her out of copper pipe, tent poles and spotty plastic sheeting (dreadful stuff to sew, I broke numerous sewing machine needles). Daisy was looking pretty amazing inside and out. Tim, who lives in the village, had brought me numerous maps and guides for castles etc. that he had collected over the years and which he very generously loaned to me.

With the help of my patient daughter Jo, I had purchased and learnt how to use a smartphone. Wow! This was going to be my main contact with all the people I loved plus my entertainment.

Daisy was packed and I was ready to go! Carol (who is one of the most thoughtful people I know) had arrived to say her farewell and presented me with a St. Christopher necklace which I had to swear never ever to take off during the whole of the trip. It was a very emotional moment. Other farewells and hugs were received and given. It was strange to think I wouldn't be seeing everyone for quite some time.

On 8th May I was ready to go and for the adventure to start...

Whatever was I doing!!!

Chapter 2

Ready to go!
The Atlantic Highway

The Atlantic Highway is a part of the A39, a stretch of road which runs through Somerset, Devon and Cornwall on the South West Peninsula described as 'remote'.

During the months of searching for Daisy, I did do a bit of planning. I didn't want to be too prescriptive and just had the idea that I would travel up one side of the country, across and down the other side with the odd foray inland. Simple! I'm ashamed to say that there were parts of this country that I didn't even know existed.

I joined the Camping and Caravanning Club (CCC) and they sent me an excellent handbook and a map showing where all of the club's sites were but also where many other sites were situated. These proved to be invaluable. I also took my National Trust Book, Great Britain's Best Trips which details 36 scenic road trips throughout the country (a Christmas present from Jenny) and a somewhat out-of-date map book. Armed with these together with a SATNAV and a smartphone I was ready to go..

Day 1

My first port of call was Mawgan Porth, a little way up the coast from Newquay. On the morning of the 8th May, as I say, Daisy was all packed up, I had locked the house and said my goodbyes to everything, got into her and nothing, she wouldn't start, her battery was flat (I did wonder if this was trying to tell me something). Jon came to my rescue again and brought over his charger which he donated to me together with a card on which he had written idiot proof instructions of how to use it (he obviously knew how clueless I am about such things). We got her going. However, something must be wrong and so back to Evil Ben's for them to check the electrics, it was more or less on my way. There was no way I wasn't going on this day as the site was booked. To use one of Richard's expressions, they checked the 'bugger's muddle' of wiring, they thought it might be the radio and so tweaked something. They would have liked to make sure but there wasn't time and I had the charger with me just in case. Not a great start to my adventure.

I left Evil Ben's at 2.30pm and found my way to The Atlantic Highway and from there I found the roads leading to Mawgan Porth. I arrived late afternoon and the sun was shining. This wasn't a club site and so not at all easy to find but I got there eventually. I wound my way down the steep, narrow, winding road leading to the cove (a good test of Daisy's brakes) and found the site on the far side very close to the beach. I parked up feeling a certain sense of achievement, what an amazing spot!

Once Daisy was going she performed well (unlike me who had crunched her gears on several occasions and got lost as usual). I had made it. I went for a walk on the fabulous beach, the tide was well out and so I could walk for some way, the sun was shining on the sea making it sparkle. I ran with my arms up to the sky, freedom, I was going to do it! I let go of all the tensions and emotions of the past weeks and days. Anyone watching would have thought I had gone mad. Only one problem, Mawgan Porth is set in a cove with steep cliffs all around it. I had promised Neil and Jo that I would call them but I couldn't get a signal and I hadn't the energy to walk up to the top of the cliffs. The radio wouldn't work either. My first night away from home and I was incommunicado. There was something rather nice about it. Having cooked a delicious omelette which I shared with a Robin that came hopping into the open door of the van and having booked the following night's site whilst consuming a small bottle of fizzy that Jo bought for me, I went to bed. A very full and busy day, I wondered what tomorrow would bring.

I awoke very early the next morning to a beautiful sunrise and just lay there listening to the birds. I reflected on how well I had slept. Daisy is very womb like and cosy and her yellow curtains make you feel bright and cheerful. I went down to the beach which was deserted as it was fairly early, such a pretty place. Time for breakfast. Before I left I got talking to the only other person on the site, he was into his second week of walking the South West Coast Path. He had been sleeping in a very small tent and he was getting all of his kit ready to continue on his journey, which he carried on his back. Already his feet were really painful and he reckoned he had another six weeks of walking to do. I thought him really brave to continue with painful feet and it made my trip seem relatively easy. He would see some amazing sights but equally (from experience of walking on the coast path) it can be pretty miserable in the rain which shows no mercy at times as you are so exposed. Having said goodbye and wishing him luck for the rest of his journey I set off for another day of exploration.

My next destination was Tintagel but I had planned various stops on the way. The coastal area between Polzeath and Widemouth Bay is a 'unique Area of Natural Beauty' and so I was expecting to see some amazing scenery.

I had my first panic-stricken moment leaving Mawgan Porth. As previously mentioned, there is a very steep road leading to it which was fine driving down but to leave you are confronted with a very steep incline and then a hairpin bend. I really wasn't familiar with how to drive Daisy and instead of taking the bend slow and wide I went up too quickly and stalled her. There I was at what felt like a 180-degree angle (a bit of an exaggeration obviously but not far off), and I had cars directly behind me and cars coming the other way and so I couldn't get the cars behind to overtake me. My heart was in my mouth, it was thumping really hard and I thought at any moment I was going to have a heart attack, I just wanted to get out and pretend she was nothing to do with me.

After taking some deep breaths and praying very hard to St. Christopher, I somehow got her going again without rolling back. I really don't know how I did it as it was by far the worst hill start I had ever had to undertake. I was just very thankful that Daisy's handbrake held (it is far less sophisticated than modern day handbrakes). Phew, that was close! It took quite some time for my heart rate to go back to normal again and in the meantime, I took a wrong turn. I was lost yet again and ended up on the A30 which wasn't part of my plan as I wanted to stay on the Atlantic Highway or travel along the back-roads keeping as close to the coast as I could. I eventually found my way back but had strayed miles out of my way.

At last I was at Rock where I stayed for a while to explore the area which seems to be a favourite place for the rich, good and great. Or should I say celebrities? (I'm not so sure about them being the good and great). It is a very pretty place but it looked quite stark when I was there as the weather had become inclement, overcast with a cold wind. You can see across the bay to Padstow, a charming small port (Rick Stein land). I found a lovely cafe and had a warming toasted teacake and coffee, one of life's small pleasures.

I continued on my way. I didn't go down into Port Isaac on this occasion, famous for where they filmed Doc Martin, as I had been there before but I went and found St. Endellion Church, ancient and just as beautiful as Sir John Betjeman had described it in his poem 'St. Endellion! St. Endellion! The name is like a ring of bells'.............. This was the first of many of the churches I visited. I find churches fascinating as they contain the history of not only the wealthy but of ordinary folk. They are a witness to all the important moments in people's lives throughout the ages and a testament to craftsmanship whether it be the building itself, the stained glass or other artefacts.

I eventually travelled onto Tintagel described as 'Cornwall's most legend-strewn location'. It is said to be the birthplace of King Arthur which I could well believe, it seemed so magical. I found the campsite I was staying on and left Daisy there and then I went off exploring. First of all, I had a wander around the shopping area and visited the Old Post Office which is a really interesting ancient stone building, the National Trust look after it now. I then found my way to the castle. I climbed the cliff-side stairs and over the bridge (not for the faint-hearted) to the castle ruins perched high on the cliffs with the sea crashing into them below. Absolutely stunning! I wandered around the ruins and tried to imagine just how it would have looked and what life would have been like living there all of that time ago. This fortress was only built in the 1300's and so it couldn't have been home to King Arthur but who knows what was on the site beforehand. Unfortunately, the tide was in and so I couldn't go and explore Merlin's Cave down below. There was definitely a feeling of ancient timelessness and magic there.

I found the local church, St. Materiana, but it wasn't in the centre of the village where I thought it would be. It is situated on top of Glebe cliff which is between Trevena and the castle. It was well worth discovering, it is quite small but it has ancient simplicity and beautiful stained glass windows. It seemed a part of the magic of the place. The coastline all around is fabulous but somehow I found the cliffs quite menacing in places and found myself pondering on how easy it would be to just step off into the foaming waters below as the waves crashed against the cliffs. A shiver ran down my spine and I stepped away feeling a sense of unease.

I'm ashamed to say that there was a time not long after Richard died that I may have been tempted but, of course, I wouldn't have done because it is never fair on family and friends and there is always a tomorrow when life seems so much better again. The feeling passed as I hurried back to Daisy, it had started to rain really hard. It rained really hard all of that evening and I thought what a horrible night the poor guy I met this morning would have in his little tent. I was very thankful for Daisy as she is very cosy and dry. I was intrigued by the couple who were parked next to me on the site. They wore matching brown overall type outfits, they reminded me of the couple who always wore matching jumpers in the comedy Ever Decreasing Circles, I found out later they were from Germany, really nice people. It was still raining hard when I turned in for the night. Another exciting and fascinating day.

Thank goodness the sun was shining again for the next part of my adventure. I left Tintagel and made my way to Boscastle to meet Heather. Heather did her curacy with us and was then given six parishes to look after, Tintagel and Boscastle being two of them. I found her recording gravestones at another of her parishes. We went back to the rectory for coffee and caught up on our news. Heather came to the priesthood late in life, she had spent sometime in the forces and on the Falklands plus she had had other careers before being called to become a priest. I have always found her to be an inspiration as she is so clever, very talented and fun. She was off to China the following day and so I was very fortunate to have found her at home. She pointed me in the direction of the harbour at Boscastle.

Boscastle is another very special place. It was difficult to picture now how it would have looked after the awful landslide and floods which they suffered a few years earlier where billions of litres of water came rushing down through the village. Today it was peaceful and calm and bathed in sunshine. I spent a happy hour or so wandering around and found a good place to sit and have an ice cream. If you are interested in witches, there is a fascinating Museum of Witchcraft and Magic in Boscastle where you are reminded that Cornwall still has its witches (white ones, I hope) and Pagan festivals are still held in places.

Heather had also told me about an excellent farm shop where I bought all sorts of delicious treats and which was quite close to my next destination, Bude.

Lost again, I had asked directions but somehow took a wrong turn and ended up in Crackington Haven, a remote tiny unspoilt coastal village. The SATNAV didn't even recognise the postcode for the site that I was looking for but I was finding that more often than not it led to the discovery of somewhere I wouldn't have found otherwise. Needless to say, I was pleased to have found Crackington Haven. Daisy was a star and coped really well with the precipitous ups and downs. I eventually found the CCC site I had booked which had stunning views out over the sea but it took me a while to find a pitch which was reasonably level. I tried to use the chocks I had bought (plastic things you put under the wheels to level a van up) but Daisy was having none of it. The site person was very patient with me and I eventually found a fairly even spot with sea views and 'docked' satisfactorily. I spent the afternoon planning where to go next and decided to head for Clovelly and then slightly inland to Umberleigh. One of the great things about the Camping and Caravanning Club is that the site office where you are staying will book the next site for you.

I awoke the next day to Daisy rocking from side to side, the downside of being on the cliff tops in a strong south westerly wind. Also my feet were dangling over the end of the bed and were freezing cold, I must have been on a slight slope after all. It was at this point that I realised I should have waited and had a new heating system fitted. However, I wasn't downhearted and I was ready for another day's adventure.

I discovered that whilst driving an old vehicle you often have a very clear road ahead of you and you start thinking the roads are very quiet but if you look in your rear-view mirror you realise that that is because the cars are all behind you. I learnt to take a run at the hills which helped but if the tail back became too great I would pull over and let the traffic pass me. Most people are very patient but you do get those who are particularly impatient and risk life and limb to overtake.

I carried on up the Atlantic Highway with a view to visiting Hartland Abbey on my way to Clovelly. Much to my great disappointment it was closed but I did find St. James the Great Parish Church at Kilkhampton where I found the internationally acclaimed amazing stained-glass windows in the Grenville Chapel designed by John Richard Clayton, which he produced to commemorate the Grenville family whose descendants played such an important part in British history.

The next leg of my journey was momentous because I was about to leave Cornwall and move into Devon.

I arrived at Clovelly and parked Daisy. You have to go through a reception area/ shop/cafe as you have to pay to go into the village but it was well worth the entrance fee. Its history goes back to the 9th century and it remains privately owned. It is still a working fishing village and donkeys and sledges are used to carry goods up and down the incredibly steep cobbled paths which are too narrow and too steep for vehicles. I really enjoyed walking down these paths with some steps leading through the village down to the harbour and admiring the different houses built on either side, some detached and some rows of pretty cottages with little alley-ways leading off. There was one cottage that had wellington boots of various sizes, full of pretty plants straddling its steps. It was wonderful to see that they were all lived in and you could tell there was very much of a community spirit there. You can walk along the harbour walls and look out to sea. Walking back up can be a bit challenging but there are lots of places where you can stop to look back and admire the view. A very unique and picturesque place, I'm not surprised so many films have been shot there. If you are unable to walk to the harbour there are vehicles which can take you via a road which leads to the hotel. You can then walk along the harbour wall and look out to sea or just sit and have something to eat at the hotel.

I was very pleased that I had chosen to include Clovelly in my adventure.

I left Clovelly and The Atlantic Highway for a while and travelled inland to another CCC site at Umberleigh. I really enjoyed my stay on this small site. I had a lovely private pitch from which I could enjoy the beautiful sunrises and sunsets and at last it was warm enough to sit outside. I arrived late afternoon and went for a very enjoyable walk by the side of the river but it was really steep coming back. I cooked the sausages for supper which I had bought from the farm shop and which were absolutely delicious (why is it even the humble sausage can taste so great when eating them outside in the fresh air?). I reckoned I had earned them after all the walking I had done that day, particularly walking back up through Clovelly, a very good test of the cardiovascular system. I had good phone reception from here as well and so I was able to catch up with family and friends.

I was staying at Umberleigh for a few days and so I could have a fairly relaxed start to the day. Day 3, and I awoke to a magnificent sunrise, a fabulous start to the day. I met a lovely couple from Sussex who had a little girl called Daisy and so my Daisy had to have her photograph taken (I was really pleased that I had called her Daisy). I had the perfect spot for people watching on this site as well as I wasn't far from the dog walking area. I came to the conclusion that it is surprising how many people do really look like their dogs.

I eventually got my act together and set off for Arlington Court, now owned by the NT but was once the home of the Chichesters. The house is Regency in style and seemed to me very homely. There is a lot to see as the Chichesters were great travellers and collectors and so the house is full of their souvenirs. The carriage collection comprises over forty vehicles and so I spent some time in there looking at all of the weird and wonderful contraptions from the 19th and 20th centuries. It includes what was once the stately coach of The Speaker of the House which was even more ornate and had more gold on it than some of the royal coaches. It made me realise how important this position in parliament was. Whilst I sat having lunch outside, a Nuthatch came to join me looking for crumbs. I know tame Sparrows, Finches and Robins are very common visitors to these places but I was so surprised by the Nuthatch as I always think of them as being very shy birds. What a joy! I spent the afternoon exploring the gardens, the Azaleas were stunning and I gained lots of ideas for what I could do with my garden (if only I had an army of gardeners to help). I sat by the lake for a while admiring the view. It was early May and the bluebells and wild garlic were just about at their best, a carpet of whites and blues with their special heady scent pervading the whole area. What must it have been like to own a house and gardens like this?

I got back to the site late afternoon, my journey back seeming much quicker than the journey there, I suspect I took a wrong turn again. What a lovely way to have spent a day. It had turned quite cold in the evening and so I just had soup for supper sat in Daisy. I rang the local vicar and he told me there was a service that Sunday at 11am in St Hieritha Church, Chittlehampton, which wasn't far away and I should be able to see its tower from the campsite.

Another leisurely start as the service didn't start until 11am. I was beginning to learn how important the shower block facilities were and how timing was all important. Some of the older campsites (not Umberleigh) still had few showers but a number of cubicles for just washing yourself, it just goes to show how times have changed. If this was the case then there would be long queues at certain times for the precious showers. Also, it is important that you make sure you have everything with you that you need as there is nothing worse than finding yourself locked in a cubicle soaking wet with no towel or no top to put on (this did happen to me). Sometimes I didn't mind queuing as it gave me the opportunity to have a chat. I wasn't queuing but I did bump into the couple from Sussex again. They had a great sense of humour and so the day started with lots of laughter, always a bonus. This was followed by my first cooked breakfast which I was able to enjoy sitting outside. I thought 'this is the life'.

I finally got my act together and drove Daisy to the Church which I could see from the campsite, except it was the wrong one, I was in Atherton, totally in the opposite direction. Why didn't I check the map book? Suddenly my relaxed morning had disappeared and I was now in a panic as I was going to be late for the service. Fortunately, I made it just in time and I parked Daisy in the very pretty tree lined square just outside the church. I dashed into the church (there is nothing worse than going in late) and found a spare pew towards the front just as the service was starting. I thought, 'phew that was close,' but I then realised I was sitting amongst a whole load of men (most unusual to find so many men at a service, certainly around my way) and looked behind to where all the women were sitting. Oops! Actually, it was a lovely service in a beautiful church and I was made to feel very welcome. I stayed and had a cup of coffee with them and enjoyed talking to the 90-year old organist who had been a music and English teacher and was married to a doctor. You really meet the most interesting people in these places. I had a wander around and found that the church had a very important history and had once been a Pilgrimage Church. This was my first encounter with the idea of Pilgrimage.

After exploring the very pretty village of Chittlehampton, I went onto the Castle Hill Gardens in Filleigh. The drive there was wonderful through the beautiful countryside, I had to pull over on numerous occasions to let pony and traps go by. I felt for a while that I had entered a time warp and gone back in time. The estate belongs to the Fortescue's and dates back to 1454, its 50-acre gardens were amazing and surrounded the 'resplendent Mansion'. I spent several blissful hours there wandering around the gardens admiring the sculptures and borders, the walled garden and then along by the river where I found more stunning Azaleas. Beautiful walks everywhere, I discovered Ugley Bridge on the walk up to the castle for example where you have views over to Exmoor and Dartmoor.

I then walked to St. Paul's Church which I think is probably one of the most beautiful small churches I have ever seen, it is so special. To mention but a few of its attributes, it has the most beautiful painted ceiling which I understand was painted by Lady Susan Fortescue in 1880, also the rounded wall behind the altar has stained glass windows depicting the stations of the cross. I sat for a while and pondered on this and that. It was magnificent. I eventually left and carried on walking.

There was just so much colour and beauty wherever you looked. When I was there the trees had their new green hues creating a lushness but I could imagine they must look truly amazing with their autumnal oranges, reds and yellows. I could also imagine how wonderful it would be to get married in The Holwell Temple, very romantic. Driving back to Umberleigh, I felt almost overwhelmed by everything I had experienced that day, what a truly beautiful area!

The following day I woke up at 5am and Daisy was absolutely freezing cold. I thought I must get out of my cosy warm bed and put the fan heater on but managed somehow to trip the electrics. I felt I couldn't cope with the situation and so I went back to bed and thought why don't I just go home but then I remembered what a super day I had had yesterday. Eventually I braved the cold and whilst shivering, my teeth chattering, I got dressed and when I investigated the electrics I had just blown a fuse and so replaced it. Things always seem much better after a cup of tea.

I left Umberleigh around 10am and headed for Lynton, a lovely drive over Exmoor. I parked in Lynton and did the Poets Walk to the Valley of the Rocks, I couldn't stop taking photographs as the scenery was breathtaking. I found a path back through the woods to Lynmouth. I wandered all around Lynmouth stopping to sit on benches to admire the view of the river and again taking lots of photographs as it was so pretty. I visited the museum depicting what had happened during the floods of 1952 showing how dreadful it was for the people who lived there then, their lives being hard enough without such a catastrophe befalling them.

However, that day everywhere looked peaceful and beautiful and I thought what a lovely place to live in. I had a treat, fish and chips for lunch, which I ate sat overlooking the sea, they tasted so good. After further wanderings I took the Lynton & Lynmouth Cliff Railway to go back up to Lynton. It is described as 'the steepest fully water powered railway in the world'. The Victorians built the cliff railway in 1888, a masterpiece of engineering, seemingly such a simple idea of using water to take the carriages up and down the very steep slope, a gradient of 500ft and it is still working today. Water from the West Lyn River fills the 700-gallon tank on the top docked passenger car and then water from the lower car is discharged until the heavier top car descends and pulls the lower car up the incline. Speed is controlled by each driver using the 'Deadman's Handle' - fascinating and very exciting. I was glad I was travelling up it and not down as I haven't got a very good head for heights. You can stop and have a coffee at the cafe at the top.

I left Lynton and headed for the next CCC site where I was staying just outside Lynton, overlooking the sea, a small but very friendly site with some great grass pitches. Grass pitches were cheaper and so with my small budget that was important. I had only booked for one night but I realised that I could go to Ilfracombe from here and catch the boat to Lundy Island where I was hoping to see Puffins and so I stayed another night.

It was a beautiful evening and so I went for a walk down through the wooded valley at the back of the campsite. It was carpeted with bluebells and primroses, releasing their heady scent in the evening sunshine and then I came upon Lee Abbey, a Christian retreat overlooking a small bay, a perfect place for a retreat. I stood watching the sun which was just beginning to set over the water, pink fluffy clouds set against a darkening blue background and reflected in the water. Heavenly! It was a steep climb back up but well worth the effort. I sat and watched as the sun continued to set over the calm sea and thought how glad I was that I hadn't gone home.

The next day was pretty eventful!

I had an early start and left Lynton in glorious sunshine but it wasn't long before I met really thick sea mist making the drive to Ilfracombe very scary as there were lots of tight bends, and ups and downs, plus I had to put Daisy's lights on which I hadn't used beforehand. I arrived in Ilfracombe in plenty of time for the boat and was advised to park on the other side of the quay.

I admired Verity, a stainless steel and bronze statue of a pregnant Amazonian figure with a sword created by Damien Hirst in 2012. She stands 20.25 (66.4ft) metres tall and is situated on the pier at the entrance to the harbour. Quite magnificent.

Time to board the boat to Lundy. We were assured the sea mist would clear but from experience I know sea mists can last for days. Unfortunately, because of the sea mist we couldn't see any of the Devon coastline, nor Dolphins or Seals, in fact you couldn't see a thing but at least the sea was calm. There was no mention in the brochure of the steep ascent to the village of Lundy when you arrived which seemed to go on for miles. I was going to go on the guided tour but it didn't take into account Jenny's Island where the Puffins breed and so I went off on my own. The island is three miles long and half a mile wide and is situated ten miles off the north coast of Devon where the Atlantic meets the Bristol Channel. It is described as an 'Area of Outstanding Natural Beauty', an 'Island of Contrasts' and 'a unique and peaceful place'. The coastline has some wonderful sounding place names such as Devil's Chimney, Kittiwake Gully, Mouse Hole and Trap. Whilst walking towards the north of the island, I met a lady called Karen and I was very grateful for her company as the mist was still really thick. We reached the north of the island and discovered the dramatic old lighthouse but could see very little. We saw the ghostly outlines of sheep and horned Highland cattle and heard Skylarks; it was certainly very atmospheric and quite eerie. We eventually found Jenny's Island but it was so enveloped in mist that you couldn't see a thing let alone a Puffin, very disappointing. We eventually got back to the village which was really interesting and I visited the church.

The island has a tempestuous history as a pirate lair and is the site of 137 shipwrecks. It was time to catch the boat to go back. I had had an amazing experience but I was disappointed not to have been able to see the island at its best as I'm sure it must be very beautiful.

This really wasn't my day!

I was pretty tired by the time I had walked back to Daisy and I was looking forward to getting back to the site and putting my feet up but lo and behold! Daisy wouldn't start, my heart sank. I checked the lights and I had definitely switched them off. I had parked off the road and I was on a slight slope and so this really helpful guy suggested that I roll her back and jump start her but of course it didn't work and then he had to find someone else to help push her back again as I was now in the middle of the road. How embarrassing! Eventually, a guy from Green Flag came to my rescue and we were on our way. By the time I got back to the site it was really late and so I had a cup of hot chocolate and went to bed. Not quite the day I had hoped for but still very interesting.

The mist had gone by the following day which turned out to be dull with rain at times. Daisy had her photo taken again by a couple who were visiting from Ohio. Two friends were staying on the site and they invited me for a coffee. Bridget had a beautiful 1972 old caravan which was fitted out in retro style like Daisy. I was so impressed as she made proper coffee from beans which she ground using a really old grinder, it was delicious. They put me to shame as mostly I just used instant; although I had my coffee pot it just seemed easier. We shared our holidaying experiences and had quite a laugh, they were two very nice people.

I left Lynton around 11am heading for Minehead, Daisy started first time, thankgoodness. I looked at the map to make sure I avoided Porlock Hill as I had a bad experience once upon a time whilst driving up it. I had taken my daughter Jo, who was twelve at the time, to Butlins in Minehead. We had a day out and I attempted to go up Porlock Hill in a very old Ford Fiesta which my father had bequeathed to me when he died, it used almost as much oil as petrol. We were getting near to the top when we appeared to be at a standstill and I had visions of us rolling back. Time seemed to stand still. Jo was terrified and so was I for that matter. We did make it but the memory lingers. I had felt quite traumatised by the experience at the time and so I didn't want to encounter that area again even if I would be going down the hill on this occasion. Having said that, it is an extremely beautiful area. The route I had chosen took me high up across the moors and even though it was raining it was still really enjoyable as the scenery was beautiful plus I had the added bonus of very little traffic and so I could enjoy sauntering along in Daisy listening to her very special engine noise and being able to look around.

On the way to Minehead, I stopped at Dunster, yet another very special place. Dunster village has a very wide street lined with beautiful old houses and it has an ancient market place plus the odd cafe and hotel. I wandered around and visited the old working watermill and also the church. The main reason for going to Dunster was to visit the castle which didn't disappoint. It stands on top of the hill where a castle has been for over 1000 years starting as a Saxon stronghold. It eventually became a comfortable Victorian home. The views from every aspect at the top are to die for. There are lots of interesting things to see but I couldn't help but admire the 17th century leather hangings depicting various scenes such as the star struck lovers, Anthony and Cleopatra. I have never seen anything like them before.

Whilst I was there, a guy was playing the piano in one of the rooms and someone else on the stairs singing, it all seemed quite magical. I would have loved to have floated down the gorgeous staircase in a beautiful gown and made the 'grand entrance'. The gardens are extensive and lovely and you can go underground to the vaulted reservoir, another feat of Victorian engineering. What an interesting and beautiful place with a fascinating history!

I carried on to find the site in Minehead where I was staying next which is situated on the top of a very steep hill overlooking the sea, Daisy took the hill in her stride. Once settled I cooked a stir fry for supper as I hadn't eaten much the day before and then I spent the evening reading and watching the baby rabbits, they were everywhere. Tomorrow I would head for Melksham and leave the Atlantic Highway.

I had only been away for just over a week but already I had travelled miles and experienced so many new things and explored some wonderful places and learnt so much more about the history of the area. I live on the South Coast of Cornwall but I had really enjoyed exploring more of the rugged North Coast, finding some stunningly beautiful and interesting places (especially Tintagel) and learning more about the history of the peoples. Celtic crosses remind you of a time gone by and wherever you look in Cornwall you can see chimneys leftover from its mining history. The geology of Cornwall's coastline is also extremely interesting.

From Cornwall I continued on and entered Devon and then on into Somerset. I had strayed from the Atlantic Highway on occasions (sometimes because I just got lost) but it had served me well when it came to exploring the coastal towns and villages and the scenery was stunning.

I wonder what will happen next!

Mawgan Porth beach

The cliffs at Tintagel taken from the bridge to the castle

Cricklehamton Church

The rounded chapel and painted ceiling of St. Paul's church

Lynton

The walk down through the woods to Lee Abbey

Dunster Castle

Chapter 3

Gower Peninsular and other places May 17th - June 8th

I should have probably done a course on navigation before leaving as I still got lost a lot plus I should, on reflection, have planned the route a bit better and become a lot more familiar with driving Daisy. However, I was beginning to get into a bit of a routine. I would wake at dawn and start the day with a cup of tea after warming Daisy up a bit with the fan heater. I would shower and have breakfast and get Daisy ready for the day, study the map to plan how I was going to get to my next destination and what I wanted to see on the way. I would drive, explore and in the evening have supper and then think about the day and write my journal. Whenever I had a signal, I would contact family or friends to let them know I was okay and where I was.

I had arranged to meet a friend, Jill, on the Gower Peninsula in a few days' time but there were places I wanted to see on the way. I headed inland, still on the A39 towards Glastonbury. I drove through some really pretty countryside and eventually reached Glastonbury where I would have stopped as it is a fascinating place but I had visited there previously. It's famous for the Glastonbury Festival, but also for Glastonbury Abbey being one of the earliest Christian Foundations to which it is said Joseph of Arimathea brought the Holy Grail. Also, it is supposed to be yet another legendary burial place for King Arthur. I remember it as quite a unique place which is steeped in witchcraft and wizards and has a lot of alternative bookshops etc. However, on this occasion I continued onto Wells.

On reaching Wells I found a car park fairly easily but then I realised that I had to go up a ramp onto the second storey as the ground floor was for supermarket shoppers only. It was really narrow but fine (or so I thought). Set on the western slopes of the Mendip Hills, Wells is the quintessential beautiful English town, or should I say, city, albeit one of the smallest, with its mellow stone buildings and shops on either side of the road leading to the cathedral which was where I was heading for.

I considered Wells Cathedral at the time to be the most beautiful I had ever seen and this view didn't change throughout my travels. I marvelled at the quality of the stonework and medieval sculptures on the front wall starting in the lower niches with biblical scenes rising through kings, bishops and orders of angels to the twelve Apostles with Christ overall but once inside, the sense of light and peace enveloped me. I wandered around almost in a trance trying to take everything in.

I decided to do the official guided tour as I wanted to find out so much more, this was well worth doing. Although a later addition in 1338-48, to prevent damage from the sinking tower foundations, the medieval scissor arches in the nave enhance rather than detract from its beauty. Each area of the cathedral has different architecture and beauty and at the same time it is very spiritual and light. The painted ceilings are just amazing. I arrived at the old clock which dates back to around 1390 and is one of the oldest clock faces in the world, just in time to see the jousting knights, fascinating. The verger said a prayer after it had finished. Also, the medieval stained glass is beautiful with the Jesse window being the crowning glory. I had visited another place of pilgrimage.

Outside of the cathedral is The Vicars' Close, it is the only complete medieval street left in England and was built for the men of the choir. The Bishop's Palace is also a lovely place to visit, it was the gardens that I liked most with a beautiful moat on which many ducks lived. I also visited the Parish Church of St. Cuthbert which again was well worth a visit. The countryside around Wells was very lush at the time and I felt bathed in history and beauty by the time I came to leave. The only blot on the day was, I scratched Daisy on the way down from the second storey of the car park. Annoyingly it was her good side as well. The ramp down, twisted and was very narrow. Fortunately, there was a guy close by who talked me through getting her down after that. I guess I was bound to do this at some point.

I was staying in Melksham overnight, a CCC premier campsite next to a canal. I had a wonderful evening walk alongside it and saw a pair of Swans with seven cygnets - wow! I didn't realise they could have that many. They definitely looked the proud parents as they glided so effortlessly along on the water in the evening sunshine surrounded by their tribe.

I attempted to eat in the pub next door to the site when I got back but they said they were full and then a couple came in after me and they said they would squeeze them in. I was a bit miffed to say the least and should have made a fuss but I was still bathed in spiritual beauty from such an amazing day that I let it go and I had a snack in Daisy instead. I guess they didn't want a single person taking up a table. It's a shame pubs don't have a communal table where people on their own can sit with others who are also on their own.

It was day ten and glorious sunshine, much warmer than it had been. I made an early start as I had a long drive ahead of me, I was going into Wales and I wanted to visit Chepstow Castle and Tintern Abbey on the way. I also had in mind to visit Bradford on Avon as it was not far away but when I saw the M4 sign I decided to leave it until another time. Daisy did so well as we got stuck in a lot of traffic and it was a hot day. Ben had installed an oil temperature gauge to ensure she didn't overheat and an automatic fire extinguisher inside the engine just in case. This would be the first time I had driven in Daisy on a motorway. When we were on the M4 she purred along until we reached the M48 which thankfully was well signposted. I found my first snag with having a left-hand drive vehicle. I had arrived at the toll booth to cross over the bridge which spans the Severn Estuary and, of course, I was on the wrong side for the cashier and so I had to get out of Daisy and walk around which held up the smooth running of the toll system. There is another bridge which I could have used but the M48 was more convenient for where I was going next. Going over the bridge into Wales was so exciting, the Bristol Channel at this point is really wide (I was very glad there wasn't a strong wind that day).

I made my way to Chepstow and eventually found the castle ruins. It was obviously a very impressive building at one time and soooo old, it has a fascinating history but I noted in my journal that I didn't really get any special vibes from it. I'm not sure what I was expecting. From here I headed for Tintern Abbey which had the opposite effect on me, also a ruin but it still had a spiritual atmosphere. Again, it must have been a really impressive building in its heyday and the remaining parts still are.

Celebrating the Wye Valley River Festival, an enormous balloon had been positioned at one end of the Abbey which was meant to represent the moon, it was landscaped according to NASA's photos of the moon and it really did look very realistic. It was really impressive as it was but it must have been extremely impressive when lit up in the evening against a dark backdrop, a moon so close you could touch it. Medieval chants were being played which created a spiritual atmosphere and an inkling into Abbey life. I was very lucky to see the display as it was going to the Commonwealth Games in Australia shortly after my visit. What a wonderful experience!

I should have had a fairly straightforward drive to the next site but I used google maps on my phone and followed the directions it gave me which was presumably the shortest route. It took me into the heart of beautiful countryside but the lanes were so narrow with very few overtaking places. I very nearly collided with a tractor which came around the bend head on at a great rate of knots. It was one of those moments when time seems to standstill and you pray. I got away with it although I did have to reverse for what seemed like miles. Another scary moment when my heart really was in my mouth.

However, I arrived safely at my next destination which was a site on a farm in the middle of nowhere near Abergavenny. I really liked this site although a bit run down. It was a quiet, beautiful spot with Pheasants and other birds everywhere, I also made friends with the farm dog. As it was a warm evening I was able to sit outside with a glass of wine, read and watch the sun go down. Tomorrow I was moving to the Gower Peninsular where I was meeting up with my friend Jill from Fowey who used to live in Mumbles and so she knew the area very well.

It was a warm and sunny morning and so I had a cooked breakfast which I ate outside. I tried to use the showers on this site which were very primitive and required a token. I tried to get them to work for ages but beyond my capability and I didn't really feel like sharing my shower with the spiders anyway and so I gave up. Daisy was again greatly admired by others on the site.

I got going eventually and headed to Pontypool and then onto the M4 heading for Swansea. I was slightly concerned about Daisy's oil temperature as it was a very hot day again but I had topped the oil up before I left and she was fine. I stopped at the services at junction 47 to have some lunch and much to my surprise everyone was speaking Welsh. It seemed so strange, I felt as though I was in a foreign country. I got back into Daisy, turned on the ignition and nothing. My first thought was that it was the battery again and so I asked various folk if they had jump leads. No, because you don't really need them these days, some didn't even know what they were. I had to ring Green Flag again and amazingly they were with me in a quarter of an hour. A young guy came who knew about old VW's, thankgoodness. He cleaned, tapped and banged something underneath and hey presto, she started again. Phew! I rang the site to let them know I would be late which they said was fine and when I explained where I was they said I was only fifteen minutes away.

I followed the directions according to the SATNAV which took me through a beautiful wetland area where I disturbed two herons and where there were sheep and horses wandering across this particularly narrow strip of road, parts of which had steep drops into bog land on either side. I had to really concentrate on where I was driving but fortunately I didn't meet anything coming the other way as I'm not sure what I would have done. It took me half an hour to get to the site and so I must have taken a wrong turn again. I hadn't planned on visiting anywhere on the way to the site but I'm glad I discovered this area. However, I was very relieved when I reached Gower and the next site, Caswell Bay. It was a huge site but I was in a field with only one other caravan and so it was fine. I could now relax for a few days as no driving. I concocted something for supper and sat and read. Daisy was starting fine again.

Jill had mentioned that this site would be a good one to book as it was close to where she was staying but in the event it was quite a way off and in fact the Three Cliffs Bay where I was going to be staying in a few weeks' time would have been nearer. However, she very kindly did all of the driving on the days we met. She arrived at 9.30, so lovely to see a friendly face and to have company. Jill has a gorgeous golden retriever called William. We went for a walk, got lost and ended up in someone's garden and so had to retrace our steps back to the site. We ended up going to Port Eynon, it reminded me a bit of Praa Sands, we walked along the beautiful sandy beach, the sea was incredibly calm. William attracts much attention and so lots of people stopped to chat (perhaps I should have brought a dog on my trip). We caught up on all our news and sat, and people watched. On the way back, Jill took a wrong turn (glad it's not just me who gets lost). We ended up doing a very scenic route back, even going to Three Cliffs Bay which was how I knew it was closer to her. We got back eventually having had a really good time, we laughed so much. I had a brilliant day, so relaxing not having to drive, I felt positively horizontal that evening. I did ring family and friends to let them know I was okay.

The following day we went into Mumbles, a beautiful town with a castle and promenade overlooking the bay, across the other side of the bay you could see the very industrial Port Talbot and Swansea. We spent the day there, Jill gave me the guided tour and she was very pleased to see that the pet shop she had started when she lived there was still thriving. We had supper where she was staying and then she drove me back along the coast to Caswell Bay just as the sun was setting. Stunning!

I had been away for two weeks and thought it was about time I did laundry and as Jill was meeting up with other friends the next day, I thought it was the ideal opportunity plus it was warm and sunny. This was the first morning that Daisy wasn't freezing cold. I stripped the bed and put it all out to air on the fence (a good job no one else was around.) I was beginning to feel like a traditional gypsy, always on the move. I gave Daisy a good clean inside and out, plus I reorganised a few things which I felt weren't working very well. I used the site laundry to wash and dry everything. This took all morning but it left me the afternoon to do further planning. I wished I hadn't pre-booked and paid for the Three Cliffs Bay site as it made the next part of my journey really difficult to sort out. I decided to divert to Hay on Wye via Brecon and then Hereford. However, I still had a few days left at Caswell Bay and seeing Jill.

Our next adventure was Rosilli where we stopped for coffee at the NT shop and then walked to the point. I understand you can walk across to the island when the tide is right out. We then carried on to Oxwich Bay where we found a beautiful 12th century church but unfortunately it was locked and so we had to make do with peering in through the windows. We had a coffee at the hotel on the beach and then drove on to Park Mill and walked to Three Cliffs Bay. Absolutely amazing. Bluebells and gorse everywhere.

Jill stopped for supper and so my first night of entertaining in Daisy. We had bought sausages from the farm shop which we had with couscous in which I had added bits of red pepper, onions, raisins etc., not my usual level of entertaining but it tasted pretty good after all the walking we had done and somehow tasted better for eating it outside in the evening sunshine. We had lots of laughs again, a fun day.

My last day with Jill was spent exploring the north of the Gower. We started off at Penclawdd but didn't stay long as it was just a mish mash of houses and businesses alongside the River Loughor and so we carried on to Llanmadoc which was lovely. There was a community shop which sold the best coffee ever and I had the most enormous piece of lime and coconut sponge cake, yummy! We took William for a walk down to Whiteford Point along the sand dunes and beach which was vast. The walk took us down through quite steep rocks which were covered in cowslips of all things. On the other side there was a marsh with bog irises, reeds, etc but also creeping willow which I had never seen before. There was also a large plantation of conifers which had been planted to stabilise the area. We explored Llangennith village. It was so funny when we drove into the village as a sheep and her two lambs were lying on the road just around a bend. We thought them in danger and so tried shooing them into a field. They led us a merry dance and so we had to give up in the end. However, as we arrived in the village there were sheep everywhere including some really cute lambs, no markings. It would appear they just roam around freely, an amazing feature of the village. We then went on to Eddies on the other side of the point, a very popular surfing area. I had said I would take Jill there for supper to thank her for all the driving she had done. Unfortunately, my idea of eating outside watching the sun go down didn't work out as it was raining by this time and the sand dunes blocked the sea view. When I got back I was surprised to find the site had been invaded, it was now really full, people everywhere, lots of families. I had to say farewell to Jill, a bit emotional as it had been such a really great week.

It was a Saturday and I decided to make the most of not driving and so I spent the day exploring on foot, the sun was shining again. However, first of all I spent some time organising super-package breakdown cover with the RAC which included an overnight stay in a hotel if necessary, I realised that my present cover was insufficient, a painful and expensive process but it had to be done. Once sorted, I headed off from the campsite to Llanmadoc, a great walk across the downs. I disturbed horses and sheep, one of the horses had a beautiful long mane which reached the floor, it was gorgeous. The sheep had red marks on them and so obviously belonged to someone unlike the ones that just meander along the road in the village. Beautiful views overlooking the marsh and bay with a lighthouse a little way out. I walked down to the Britannia Inn where I had a fantastic lunch sat in the garden, a delicious ham and salad roll which came with chips, great, but not so great when it came to walking back up the hill as I was so full. I did a detour as I spotted a signboard in amongst some trees at the top of the hill referring to the remains of an old school building from I think, 1850-1935. The school closed because it had no heating, the poor children must have been frozen as it is in a very exposed position. There were photographs on the board of the Head with her various classes. Life must have been very hard then. Talk about serendipity, this had been a wonderful interlude to my walk. It was very hot when I got back to the site and so I had an ice cream and sat outside and read. Only one more day and then back on the road.

It was a Sunday and I planned to go to the 11.15 service at Llanrhidian and so I had to drive again. I was a bit early but the lovely Church Warden, Margaret, told me about the church and, in particular, its saint. Apparently, he had one leg and was rescued and raised by seagulls, what a wonderful story. The vicar was very charismatic and I felt very uplifted by his sermon, the church was very welcoming. It was the anniversary of Richard's death and so I lit a candle and wondered what he would have made of all this? After the service I carried on down the lanes and parked not far from Eddies. I had to pay £3 but it was worth it as there was easy access to the beach through the sand dunes. The tide was well out and so I was able to walk for miles. I found an enormous jelly fish on the beach, I certainly wouldn't have wanted to meet up with it in the sea, plus there were also literally hundreds of empty razor bill shells. I spotted a flock of small Sand Pipers - they can run along the sand like the clappers and then take off in perfect unison. When I got back to the site they thought I had left, a mix up over the booking, fortunately my space was still vacant. However, I had to move later to another pitch. I was glad to be leaving there.

An early start!

A great drive to Hay-on-Wye. Another hot day and so a bit worried about Daisy's oil temperature. It did go up to just below the 100 mark but not above, thankgoodness, she went like a dream. I took my time driving through the Brecon Beacons and Black Mountains as so stunningly beautiful, it seemed very special. I stopped at Tretower on the way to Brecon, an incredibly old medieval dower house, it replaced the castle which was Norman. You can still walk around the castle ruins and you can explore most of the house. The kitchens and banqueting hall really give a flavour of how life would have been then. The gardens are lovely and I spent some time just sitting in them soaking up the atmosphere of the place.

My next stop Brecon. I hadn't appreciated that Brecon has a cathedral. When I visited they were working on the outside and I couldn't really see how it looked but the inside was lovely. The thing I remember most about it was this enormous cross made from driftwood hanging down from the bell tower which was extremely high up. It also has a beautiful stained glass window. I wandered around Brecon itself. It has a castle which has been made into a hotel. It also has another church, St. Mary's, one aisle of which has been turned into a coffee house. An enjoyable afternoon wandering around a lovely old town, well worth the visit. I went on to find the next camp site at Hay-on-Wye.

I really liked this site at Borders Hideaway. I met a lovely couple, Nigel and Ann, who had a really beautiful orange/white VW Bay Campervan. We had a great chat about vans and they were telling me about some of their campervan experiences which were pretty hair raising, one of which included a happening with a bear in Canada. Nigel loaned me his book on the history of the VW Van by Mike Harding and in it there was a picture of Daisy! I couldn't believe it! It was exactly the same colour and had an identical interior, it then dawned on me that she was an original. Somehow this only enhanced my growing feelings for her despite her not always starting as she should.

The next morning I thought I would drive Daisy into town. It should have taken me ten minutes to get to the town from the camp site but I again took a wrong turn and found myself on the way to Hereford. I had to turn around but I then discovered that I could pay £1 and cross over to Hay-on-Wye on a very old wooden bridge, all very exciting. The bridge reminded me of a novel I had read some time ago by Barbara Erskine, called Sleepers Castle which was set just outside of Hay-on-Wye. I could imagine two of the characters from the book, Catrin and Joan, crossing over this same bridge on their horses to get to Market Day in Hay in the 1400's. Fanciful, I suppose, as I can't imagine the bridge was actually that old.

The town is just as I remembered it, a really pretty old town with hundreds of bookshops and other lovely individual shops and, of course, its castle. I hadn't planned on going to the Hay-on-Wye Literary Festival but it just so happened that it was on whilst I was there. When I went to the Festival many years ago, I'm sure the events were held in various venues around the town but much to my amazement it has now turned into a very grand affair and it takes place on a festival field with huge marquees elaborately fitted out inside with wooden walkways etc. There were hundreds of people milling around, I was staggered to see how popular it had become.

I bought a programme and decided there were two events that I wanted to see and managed to get tickets for both. The first was free as it was in the BBC tent. They were recording a programme for Radio 3 called The Essay. Two writers chose their favourite fictional female character to talk about, one chose Orlando and the other Jane Eyre. Both were very good and very funny, really enjoyable. The second was to see Salman Rushdie and Tishani Doshi In Conversation. This was excellent, funny but at the same time they made some very valid points. I left the Festival feeling very stimulated.

I spoke to Neil in the evening as he was starting a new job and I wanted to wish him Good Luck. Next stop, Hereford.

The next day I set off with a view to visiting Hereford Cathedral. I found somewhere to park albeit really expensive, £6 extortion! What an incredible place the cathedral is!! My first impression was one of strength and that this red brick building was built to last forever. Inside, the pillars are of grey stone and vast, this supported my first impression that it was built with the intention that the cathedral would never fall down. It also has a very interesting heating system. However, as amazing as the building is, it is its contents that I was really taken aback by. This was the first time I had ever seen a chained library which really made me understand how important early books were. The endeavour that went into writing and producing them and which form the bedrock of our education and understanding of the world, a lot of which we now take very much for granted. From the chained library I found my way to the Mappa Mundi exhibition which was also extremely interesting and very well done. What an extraordinary history this island has had! It was quite amazing to see how the world was perceived at the time when the map was drawn up and to think it was done on animal skin with quills, etc and still survives. I felt very humbled by the experience and very much more in touch with the past and the peoples who have populated this island for generations.

The next site was a CCC site near Hereford situated between Hereford and Ledbury and I would never have found it but for Google Maps. It has a lake and so attracts a lot of fishermen. I had a splendid pitch overlooking the lake which has reeds and bog irises around it which were out at the time, really beautiful. I could watch the ducks with their ducklings, very amusing, and a pair of geese. The site also had excellent facilities, really good showers and shop where I was able to purchase WD40 which enabled me to sort out my wing mirror which was stuck in a wrong position for motorway driving. The reason for staying on this site was to meet up with my friend Ann from Pershore in Ledbury.

A number of the CCC sites have bus stops outside and so rather than drive I took the bus into Ledbury. I met up with Ann as we had arranged and we had a quick look around the town and then had lunch so we could catch up on all our news. She left after lunch but both Ann and Pete were joining me the next day in the Forest of Dean. I spent the afternoon wandering around Ledbury. The Church of St. Michael and All Angels was massive for such a small town but it was built to accommodate people from the wider area. Anyway, it was vast and beautiful with a separate tower housing eight bells. A special treat, the organist was playing and so I sat and listened to him for a while. I also visited the Master's House (library) and the painted room (part of the council buildings) and the Butchers Museum all housed in Tudor buildings. Really interesting. Apparently, Ledbury was quite a poor town after the plague hence so many Tudor buildings remain as there was no money to update them which makes Ledbury a pretty special place.

By the time I got back to the site it was thundering and lightning. I hadn't considered how it would feel to sit in a tin box with dramatic flashes, bangs and torrential rain which sounded more like hail stones hitting the roof. I confess to feeling very alone and just a little frightened at times. Fortunately, it had stopped by bed time. I would have liked to spend another night there but it was time to move on.

I stopped off at Ross on my way and had a look around the town. I didn't feel it was as pretty as Hay or Brecon or Ledbury but I suppose I had been spoilt by these lovely towns and so standards were being set high. I inevitably had a look around the church which was well worth the visit. Apparently it had trees growing in it at one time but was very well kept now. I arrived at the site in the Forest of Dean via a route which the site information warned you not to take. However, although very narrow in places it was nothing compared to some of the roads I had been on and it was very pretty. Amazingly, Ann and Pete arrived at the same time as me. I stopped at the check in office and there they were right behind me and we had pitches next door to one another which was great. We did a four mile walk through the woods to the river and back which was beautiful. We had tea but then seamlessly moved on to the G & T's and then Ann cooked salmon, asparagus, new potatoes and broad beans which was followed by strawberries accompanied by a very delicious wine. You may find it strange that I should go into so much detail but after eating very little, I felt as though I had had a banquet as this was the most I had eaten since I left home. By the time Pete got out the single malt for night caps, Ann and I were pretty sozzled but it had been really good fun.

The following day was glorious, sunny with blue skies but with a bit of a breeze. Perfect walking weather. We had a slow start due the previous evening but then set off for the day's walk. We left the site and walked past a log cabin which was part of a complex. It had a cafe and really good shop, we thought we would eat there in the evening. We found the local church which had become more of a community centre. It was at this point that we realised we were heading in the wrong direction but fortunately Pete had a gadget which got us back on track. We followed a stream which ran through the woods for some way which contained newts, tadpoles and water boatmen. We saw squirrels and evidence of wild boar.

We eventually arrived at the view point high above Symonds Yat. Wow! Fantastic! Such an incredible view of the valley and the Wye. The RSPB had a telescope there to watch the Falcons which were nesting in holes in one of the rocks. Unfortunately, we didn't see them but we did see a Buzzard. We made our way down the really steep path (I was glad I wasn't trying to walk up it) to the cafe where we stopped for lunch, they did delicious baguettes. We watched people in their canoes and the boatman who operated the rope ferry which goes backwards and forwards across the river. We used this to get across the river and I have to say the guy who was operating it must have been very fit. You sit in the boat and then he pulls you across with a rope which is tied to the other side. We walked alongside the river until we got to the rope bridge where we crossed back over. I found this pretty scary but fun, only six people are allowed on it at any one time. On the way back to the site we spotted deer and encountered a squirrel happening, there were at least three of them on the ground in undergrowth making a very strange sound indeed. Goodness only knows what was going on. By the time we got back to the site we had completed 9.7 miles (I can say that with great accuracy due to Pete's gadget). After the evening meal Pete made us a night cap and then I fell into bed. Another very special day.

Ann and Pete were off to Glastonbury for a couple of days and I was moving on to a farm at Caerleon as a stop off on my way back to Gower. Before leaving Pete had a look at my SATNAV for me as it wasn't recognising a lot of the postcodes. He suggested using the co-ordinates of map ref. instead. When I came to look for the next site reference, lo and behold, there wasn't one.

The journey started off okay, I found the road to Monmouth and went merrily along that for some time and found the sign for Usk which I was meant to be taking but the road was closed and so I had to continue to the main Newport roundabout and then come back up the other way. Google maps kicked in again but took me on a very convoluted route up cycle lanes. At one point Daisy had to go up a really really steep hill over the top and back down again - it felt as though we were on a roller coaster. After going for what seemed like miles I decided to ignore what I was being told and when I saw a sign for Caerleon I just took it. However, it became obvious after a while that I was lost. I stopped and asked a young couple if they knew the farm I was trying to get to and they said it was very complicated but they would get on board Daisy and take me there which they did. It was really kind of them, they saved the day.

I didn't really know anything about Caerleon and so when I planned this stop I had no intention of exploring but I had a special treat in store for me. Caerleon was once an old Roman port and they had uncovered Roman baths and amphitheatre there. The amphitheatre was in use and so I couldn't look around it but I did get to have a look at the baths which were so interesting. It was a shame I didn't have another day here as there was so much to see. Coming back, I found a church which had Sung Evensong at 6pm on a Sunday and I could hear the choir practising, they sounded absolutely amazing and so I stopped and waited for the service. I really enjoyed it, the singing was incredible, it was like being at a cathedral Evensong. I walked back to the site feeling very uplifted and sat outside until the sun went down as it was such a lovely evening.

It was Monday 4th June and not a good day. When I woke up I had an extremely swollen and painful nose, I had been bitten by a horsefly. I dreaded to think what I looked like. I didn't dare take antihistamine as they can make me feel drowsy and so I had to make do with cream. Things only got worse! It was my intention to visit Castle Coch on the way back to Gower and I entered the postcode for it into the SATNAV but it directed me down the wrong street and so I tried to turn around in an area which looked like a pull-in but joined someone's drive. Anyway, I backed-up and heard a crunch. I forgot about the tow-bar on the back of Daisy which sticks out quite a way and had gone into the caravan which was parked on their drive. Oops! I knocked on the door to tell the owner what I had done and the lady of the house was lovely but her husband wasn't there and so I left my telephone number. She did tell me that the SATNAV was taking me along the back lanes and I would be better off going on the M4 and follow the signs from there which I did. It was quite a way off the M4 and when I arrived at the gate to the castle it was closed. It wasn't a very grand entrance and so I went further on in the hope there may be another but I didn't find one and so had to turn around and go back. When I arrived at the gate again, there was a lady putting a sign up saying the castle was closed that day as they were having some work done on it. It really just wasn't my day. By this time my nose was really throbbing and so I was feeling pretty fed up. I found my way back onto the M4 and eventually reached the Three Cliffs Bay site.

As mentioned previously, it was a site I had pre-booked because in an article I had read it mentioned that there were amazing views and the toilet blocks were fantastic. I was so disappointed when I arrived as my pitch was next to the toilet blocks and I felt dwarfed by all these enormous campervans, there was no view at all, I just felt like I was in a goldfish bowl. In the evening the lights came on for the toilet blocks and so really bright. What a crap day: I had a throbbing nose, I had backed into a caravan which I could imagine would be a very expensive mistake, Castle Coch was closed which I had driven miles out of my way to see and now I had come back to Gower because of a site which I thought would be special and was in fact the worst I had stayed on.

However, things looked brighter the next morning. I had a walk around the site and it was true the views from the cliff across the bay were amazing and the vans that had pitches adjacent to the cliffs did have magnificent views. I also found that there was a field with tents and smaller vans pitched there and so I asked if I could move. It wasn't a problem and I was much happier there. It was also true that the showers were the best I had encountered, it was like having your own private bathroom, my view of the site changed a lot especially as it had a very good shop. A mum introduced me to her little girl called Daisy and asked if she could have her photo taken with my Daisy, she was so sweet. I was thrilled as once again my Daisy had her photo taken.

Although I felt that I had made a huge mistake coming back here it made for a relaxing couple of days because I now knew the area and could go off walking for miles and the weather was perfect, warm and sunny with a gentle breeze. The walks were pretty strenuous as so up and down but very beautiful. One day I opted to walk from the site to Oxwich Bay which was described as a moderate 6 miles. However, as usual I got lost and ended up walking too far inland and so had to backtrack. I eventually ended up in the bay and had lunch at the hotel. I would have got a taxi back as I was so tired but there wasn't one and so I had to walk. I was rewarded as I walked back through a beautiful wildlife area, so many different varieties of wild flowers including Orchids in abundance. By the time I got back my legs were like jelly. I got my deckchair down from the roof rack and that was it for the rest of the day. There were lovely country views from the field and it was very peaceful. I had a call from the person whose caravan I had backed into. I felt really awful as he explained it was up for sale. I could only apologise profusely and said I would pay for the damage. He was actually very nice about it and it was left that he would do his best to get it repaired at a reasonable cost.

It was time to start thinking about leaving this truly beautiful area which I felt I now knew fairly well and had come to love. I planned the next stage of my journey which would lead to me into Pembrokeshire.

Wells Cathdral *Scissor Arch*

Tintern Abbey and the amazing balloon

Beautiful Three Cliffs Bay

*The Chained Library
Hereford Cathedral*

Symonds Yat

Chapter 4

Pembrokeshire and Cardiganshire
June 8th – June 18th

The drive from the Gower Peninsular into Pembrokeshire went amazingly according to plan. I decided not to use the SATNAV but had planned the route using various maps. On the way I stopped off at Kidwelly to look at the castle and church there. A very interesting place. It was easy to park and when I asked a gentleman the way to the castle he said he would take me there. Carol would have been appalled that I went off with a strange man having warned me prior to leaving that I wasn't to trust anyone. However, he was just being very helpful and at my age I felt quite safe.

The castle is a ruin but a very well preserved one and there is enough of the castle left to enable you to see quite clearly what it would have looked like originally. I think I let my imagination run away with me because I was in one of the rooms and I definitely felt that something really bad had happened there, it gave me goose bumps and I had to leave immediately. St. Mary's Church was lovely, quite simple but has beautiful stained glass windows. I spent quite some time sat there in the peace and quiet, contemplating what could have happened in the castle and praying. I had visited a number of castles but this one seemed particularly bleak somehow. I guess they were built in a very turbulent time when the English and Welsh were constantly fighting one another and so it only stands to reason that during the fighting awful things would have taken place. At this point in time my prayers were very focused on the loss of Richard, my brother John, and a best friend (all had died in the last two years) and also for the rest of my family and friends.

I continued on my way to Carmarthen where I stopped for a while to have a look around. The next site was situated outside Tenby, a small but lovely site set in a wooded valley. Opposite there was an old iron works which was well worth investigating. You could easily imagine the intense heat and noise that would have been deafening when the foundry was in operation. I walked alongside the river to the beach and through a really spooky tunnel to Saundersfoot. The tunnel was quite dark and long, it was used in the past by the railway to take ore to the harbour, it must have been quite an operation at one time. However, it now offers easy access for walkers and cyclists to reach Saundersfoot. I suppose I must have walked six or seven miles.

The next morning I awoke to the sound of a Thrush singing its heart out, a Peacock joined in and then a Cockerel. What a lovely way to start the day! It was a little way into the town and so I caught a bus which very conveniently stopped outside the campsite, it went all around the houses but I wasn't in a rush. I soon realised why Tenby was such a popular holiday destination, I loved it. Some of its town walls are still standing, it is a beautiful town with lovely shops and there is so much to see and do. At its heart is its beautiful church, another St. Mary's. You could tell it was a very much loved and cared for building. It had carpeted steps leading up to the altar and the ceilings were painted in different designs. I bought a book from there based on a ghost story set around Tenby, they were selling them to raise money for Christian Aid. You can do guided walks around Tenby including 'The Ghost Walk of Tenby' which I'm sure would have been great fun to go on but unfortunately there wasn't one planned whilst I was there. I visited the harbour, RNLI Station, Museum/Art Gallery and The Merchant's House dating back to Tudor times. They were all very interesting and I learnt a lot about the history of Tenby, a very wealthy trading port at one time. There are lovely walks across the cliff tops looking down on the beautiful beaches. I walked up to the castle ruins where there is a statue of Prince Albert and a Victorian band stand down below. I wandered back into town and treated myself to a delicious meal in a restaurant next to The Merchant's House. My budget for the trip was pretty limited and so I only ate out occasionally. I then joined the throng of folks sat on benches in the sunshine and ate my ice-cream like a proper tourist. What a friendly, buzzy atmosphere Tenby has, I had had a splendid day. I caught the bus back to the site and spent the evening sat outside reading my new book, a perfect end to a brilliant day.

A glorious sunny warm day and time to move on again, heading for St. Davids with a stop at Solva on the way. I had planned the route using map books again which worked very well. Daisy had been behaving herself and so I was gaining confidence in her again, in fact I was loving driving her. Solva is a very pretty little town by the sea, just a few houses, shops, coffee places and the Solva Woollen Mill, the oldest working woollen mill in Pembrokeshire specialising in weaving flat woven floor rugs and runners using the traditional looms. I had the most delicious Welsh Cake I had ever had in one of the coffee shops there, it was warm and buttery and had cinnamon in it, yummy.

Solva has a natural harbour where you can find the remains of lime kilns. The tide was well out when I was there and so the small boats were stranded on the sand, very picturesque, a delightful place. It was a lovely drive from Solva along the coast to St. Davids. I found the CCC site but I was a bit early and so there was no one there, there was a note on the door of the office saying which pitch I had and so I went and found it but to my dismay it was in the centre of the site and on quite a slope. I was really hoping I could change it later.

I went off into St. Davids to explore and found the cathedral where I was hoping to go to Evensong at 6pm. I had found the cathedral nestled in a sheltered valley, it was built on the site of the monastery founded by St. David, Patron Saint of Wales hence its importance. It seemed to me wandering around the cathedral that it has churches within a church. The floors slope slightly and it has lots of different beautiful ceilings, some painted, some vaulted and the one area has an exquisitely carved wooden ceiling. It looks as though it has been extended at various times throughout its history. Again, you can tell how important the cathedral was in times past, as at one time two pilgrimages to St. Davids was equal to one pilgrimage to Rome. The surrounding area is beautiful, there is a stream with a bridge across and the ruins of the Bishop's Palace. The city is lovely but tiny, more like a village. I decided not to stay for the service as it was said 'Evensong' and I was really tired by the time I had wandered around and I wanted to sort out moving on the site.

The warden was there when I got back but the site was full and so I had to stay where I was. He said, "I will help you to use your levellers," my heart sank. Since the last debacle I had been watching people using them and they made it seem very easy and so I thought I would have another go. When Richard and I stayed in Kioni on Ithaca we stayed in a house right on the harbourside and in the evening we would sit outside and watch the flotillas as they started to come in to moor up. Some experienced skippers made it look so easy, they just glided in effortlessly. However, you could always tell the less experienced sailors because they would go backwards and forwards several times, bump into the other boats, get their ropes and anchors tangled up and the more things went wrong, the more they shouted at each other. It was so funny to watch. I mention this because it was my time to cause amusement. I had placed the chocks where the warden told me to and he then proceeded to give me instructions. I must have tried to get it right loads of times and the more exasperated he got with me the worse it became until eventually I reversed up and over the top of them and got them stuck underneath Daisy by which time steam was coming out of the poor man's ears. It was at this point I said I would give up and put up with the slope for the sake of his sanity and mine. He was mighty relieved. I retrieved the battered chocks and threw them up onto the roof rack never to be taken down again, evidence of my ineptitude for reversing onto the damn things.

Apart from the embarrassment of providing entertainment for the site, I really liked it there as it was so friendly. That evening a lovely couple, Cathy and Nigel from Derbyshire, invited me to their van for coffee liqueurs. We chatted for quite some time, they were off to Three Cliffs Bay the next day and so I was able to advise where to go and what to see. Equally they advised me of a lovely site to stay near Aberystwyth overlooking Cardigan Bay. They invited me to stay with them on my way up country, they were lovely people and really kind.

One of the aims on this trip was to see Puffins and as I was thwarted on Lundy I thought I would try again and so the next day I went back into St. Davids to book to go over to Skoma Island, and hang the expense! I joined the others and caught the shuttle bus down to the Old Life Boat Station waiting to embark. There was a lot of discussion going on among the staff who were in a huddle and eventually they announced that it was too windy to go. I couldn't believe it, not again! However, this gave me spare cash to spend and yesterday I only got a flavour of the city and so I now had more time to explore. I bought postcards to send to my grandchildren and went back to the area by the cathedral and sat on a bench to write them, it was sunny but I admit, quite windy. Children were playing in the stream which reminded me of when Neil and Jo were young. It was really busy with lots of holidaymakers milling around. I went back into the cathedral and wondered if it now counted that I had done two pilgrimages, I suspect not.

This was one of those days when I felt intensely lonely. People were either in couples or part of a family and obviously enjoying themselves. I had found that it was the same on the campsites, very few people seemed to travel alone especially not women.

Whilst wandering around I had spotted a delicatessen and so I spent some of the money I had been reimbursed for the sea trip, on a very expensive bottle of wine, artisan bread and blue cheese plus I treated myself to a lamb chop from the butchers. Some days I ate hardly anything but I made up for it on others. When I got back to the site I got chatting to a couple who had a white VW Bay a bit older than mine. They were from the Isle of Wight and had had many happy times in their camper. There is always a great camaraderie between fellow VW owners.

The lanes around the site were very narrow and so I decided to have a rest from driving on my last day there and instead walked from the site to the beach and then onto the Blue Lagoon. It is a spectacular deep water inlet caused by quarrying the stone from the cliff and then they blasted the cliff to let the sea water in creating a really deep and blue lagoon. Wow! The ruins of the old buildings are still there. I sat and watched three lads, two older and then, I assume, a younger brother. The two older lads were jumping off a high point into the lagoon. You could tell the youngest was really terrified as I would have been but with the persuasion of the older boys he eventually did it. I was full of admiration for him and all ended well but I was concerned for them all as it looked really dangerous. On my way back I stopped and had an ice-cream which I ate on the beach.

By this time Daisy was beginning to develop a few niggles. She has a pop-up top which is really useful when cooking as it allows you to stand up, the only thing is you do have to be careful not to bang your head on the roof when you move around (I did it a few times and it does hurt). Unfortunately, when I came to putting the top down after cooking the lamb chop, one of the clips came off, the plastic pull with the clip attached had perished. I had spotted a garage not far from the site and so before moving on again I went to see if they could replace it. Of course it was a specialist part and so I had to make do with cable ties, they gave me a large bundle to keep me going throughout the trip which was very helpful of them and they didn't charge me. Also, when I put the brake on going down a hill, sometimes the indicator came on for a few seconds. It was one of those really annoying intermittent faults but nothing too serious. I guess I had already driven hundreds of miles and so something like this was bound to happen with a very old van.

St. Davids Peninsular is described as 'A place of beauty, Peace and Pilgrimage' and I wouldn't disagree with that. The coastline is fabulous. I had spent a wonderful few days there.

On my way to my next destination, Cardigan Bay, I checked Daisy's tyre pressures and filled up the windscreen washer. In a modern car you just lift the bonnet, locate the washer bottle and fill it up, hey presto! done. Nothing so simple with Daisy. The filler point is located inside down by the pedals, when you take the lid off it releases the air pressure and so after putting the screen wash in you have to put air back in through a connector in the same way you would blow up a bicycle tyre. It isn't difficult but fiddly and makes you realise how far car design has come.

I really enjoyed the drive to the next site, it was along the beautiful Pembrokeshire coast looking out to Cardigan Bay. I had toyed with the idea at one point of taking the ferry from Fishguard to Ireland but on reflection thought it a step too far with the amount of time I had left for the trip and so I discarded the idea. I stopped at Newport instead and really enjoyed a walk around the bay and then had lunch at the Castle Inn. I ordered the starter of warm duck salad, it was such good value. When it arrived it must have been half a duck breast with potatoes, salad and a walnut dressing, absolutely delicious and only £4.25 then, but I suppose it would be more now. I arrived at the CCC site just this side of New Quay late afternoon. It was a large site but I had a really nice private pitch overlooking the countryside and protected by a hedge but more importantly it wasn't on a slope. Phew! This was just as well because it was very windy and despite the hedge I still woke up around 2.30am as Daisy was rocking from side to side again, the wind really howling and torrential rain the sound of which was unbelievable on the tin roof. It went on all night and was pretty frightening at times but I fared better than those in tents. At last the storm abated and it turned out to be a really sunny day.

I have always been a great fan of Dylan Thomas and Under Milk Wood. I know he was a flawed character in some ways (aren't we all?) but it surprises me that Wales doesn't celebrate him more than they do as I think he was something of a genius. I walked from the site into New Quay where Dylan Thomas lived for a while and where he was supposed to have based the characters of Under Milk Wood. As I was moving around the town, some of the characters came to life in my imagination as I was remembering the story e.g. Dai Bread

Dai Bread, the town baker, Mrs. Dai Bread two, his second wife, Miss Myfanwy Price who is in love with Mr Mog Edwards though they have never met, Lily Smalls, and Nogood Boyo who fishes in the bay dreaming of Mrs Dai Bread Two and geishas, just to mention but a few of them, it was so funny and very clever. I could picture it all. A fantastic experience.

By lunchtime I was ready for fish and chips which I ate overlooking the beach where dogs were allowed, it was great fun watching them have such a good time, two beautiful golden Labradors were running in and out of the sea and chasing balls and others were just chasing round with unbounded energy enjoying their freedom. One of them reminded me very much of Bertie. By the time I had to go it had become really hot and I toyed with the idea of catching a bus back to the site but I then felt I should walk the fish and chips off and so armed with a bottle of water I made my way back to the site. It was really hard work and seemed much longer than on the way. I was so grateful when I saw the site as I was really tired and my feet ached. I suppose I had walked ten miles altogether but it seemed longer as it was so hot and it was all uphill on the way back. I spent the evening sat outside reading and catching up with family and friends as I hadn't had a signal at the other site. Another lovely day.

Next stop, Aberystwyth and so not far to go. I stopped off at a NT property on the way, Llanerchaeron Gardens. The house was fairly modest by NT's standards but really interesting. It was set in beautiful woodlands with a river flowing through them. They had an exhibition on whilst I was there celebrating women's influence on this house and others like it. We forget that it was only around one hundred years ago that women got the vote and prior to that many women weren't allowed to own land in their own right. We have come a long way since then thanks to these women. The house was designed by Nash and apart from the house it had an area of buildings set around a cobbled quadrangle which housed the kitchens, cheese making rooms etc. Standing there you could really sense the banter and laughs that would have gone on when the servants were working. The lake and gardens were gorgeous and I spent a long time exploring them.

I found the turn off to the next site easily but the lane leading to it was of the sort I had had nightmares about before leaving. It was one car width and it had very few overtaking places plus it seemed to go on forever. I did meet a 4 x 4 but he very kindly reversed for me and he had to go back miles, I was so grateful. It was worth the scary moments though as the site was just as lovely as Nigel and Cathy had said and I had a pitch overlooking the whole of Cardigan Bay. I sat and watched a pair of Red Kites hunting right in front of me with the sea as a backdrop. I tried to capture the moment on camera but the shot I got was very disappointing. It was a really thrilling moment though as I had never seen one so close before, they have a huge wing span. I also spotted a Peregrine Falcon hunting a bit farther along.

As I was looking out of the window at the bay whilst cooking a stir fry for supper and watching the sun go down over the sea, I realised what a privilege it was to be doing this adventure even if it was scary and lonely at times.

I had booked to go on the Vale of Rheidol Railway today, a steam railway which runs from Aberystwyth up to Devils Bridge and so I got up bright and early as I was so excited and even the rain didn't dampen my enthusiasm. I arrived at the station early so that I could enjoy the build-up and atmosphere prior to getting on the train. It was quite a small steam engine but beautiful. I had chosen to sit in an open carriage behind the engine (it did have a roof though) and I was glad I did as I really got a feel for everything the old steam trains are loved for, that special smell of the sooty smoke, the hiss of the steam and the rhythm, the clackety clack as it chugs along the tracks. Every now and again the driver would blow the whistle. The train meanders through the Rheidol Valley and the scenery was stunning even on a dull day. It follows the path of the river but the track was built into the hillside and so for most of the way you look down from 100's of feet up, down into the valley below. The train chugged its way up and we eventually reached Devils Bridge (three bridges built one on top of the other). I took photos of the falls but didn't go down as I only had an hour there and I was desperate for a coffee. The hour went very quickly and then it was time to get back on the train for the descent which was equally as breathtaking.

Aberystwyth was the largest town I had explored in some time and so I made the most of being able to go to the bank, pharmacy etc. I walked from one end of the town to the other and even though it was raining and cold it was enjoyable. I had hoped to visit the church but there was a wedding taking place in it. Poor souls, a horrid day for a wedding but I expect they made the most of it.

I got back to the car park and would you believe it? Daisy wouldn't start again. I called the RAC. Whilst I was waiting a couple who were parked next to me in a very beaten up old VW offered to help. He had jump leads. I explained that the last time it happened it wasn't the battery but he said he would have a go. Needless to say, nothing happened but it was kind of him to try. Eventually someone from the RAC came to look at her and got her going again and explained that it was the starter motor, she needed a new one. This was the first time anyone had mentioned anything about her starter motor but it did make sense that it was what was causing the problem as each time the mechanics had banged and bashed her in the area of the starter motor. Oh dear!

That evening the rain became even heavier as I sat watching people arriving at the site for the weekend and then trying to put up their tents in the really strong wind with the rain pelting down on them. I was once more very thankful for Daisy. It was bad enough having to venture up to the site toilets. I had this wonderful position looking out to sea but I couldn't see a thing. It was the sort of evening when the grey sky meets the grey sea making it hard to detect where one starts and the other finishes. As I was sitting there I thought 'what am I going to do about Daisy and her starter motor?' I decided that provided she started okay the next day, I would continue on my way to the next site and then try and get Daisy sorted whilst I was there.

I had read that this site was perfect for spotting Dolphins which frequented Cardigan Bay and so I woke up very early the next day in the hope that I could see some. I had heard that the early morning was the best time to spot them. I had my binoculars at the ready but unfortunately it was a really horrible cold wet morning and so I could hardly see anything let alone Dolphins. I did see another Red Kite though.

Despite the awful weather I had enjoyed my time here, the pitch was so close to the sea and the steam train ride was amazing.

I was really looking forward to exploring more of Wales.

Kidwelly Castle

The bay at Solva

Rheidol Railway

Just one of the many beautiful ceilings in St. Davids Cathedral

Chapter 5

The Llyn Peninsula, Snowdonia and Anglesey June 18th – June 29th

I had planned to stop off at Harlech on the way to Pwllheli but I didn't dare just in case I couldn't get Daisy going again even though she started first time when I came to leave. The A487 took me through absolutely fabulous and stunning countryside, it even looked amazing in the rain especially driving through the mountains. There were a lot of ups and downs but Daisy coped fine although I did have to stop on a number of occasions to let the tail back of cars overtake me. I took the A470 which led me to Porthmadog as I wanted to have a look around but when it came to it, again I didn't dare stop. It took me about three and a half hours to get to my next destination, Llanystumdwy near Pwllheli. This was another CCC site but not quite so nice as the others. It was fairly close to the road and the laundry facilities weren't very good. However, I did manage to find a garage close by but it wasn't at all easy to locate as it was hidden behind a petrol station. I had to do some really tricky manoeuvres to get to it but by now I was getting used to Daisy's capabilities. The owner of the garage was very helpful and after jacking Daisy up they found the serial number for the starter motor which they had to order in but they said it would be there by tomorrow. Phew!

My morning wait to hear from the garage wasn't wasted as I planned the next part of the journey. I booked extra days on this site as I wanted to visit Harlech, Portmeirion and the rest of the Llyn Peninsula before moving on to Anglesey. I eventually got a call from the garage around 3.30pm to say they had the part and so I went back to the garage. After what seemed like an age I was told they had sent the wrong part and so they had to put the old starter motor back on. Oh well! I did some shopping on the way back and had a cook-up in the evening. It was still really horrible, cold and wet and so I spent the evening reading. The one good thing about this site, I could get radio 4 and so I was able to catch up on the Archers. The other good thing was they had several Mills and Boon books in their library. I have always pooh poohed them but they were the perfect easy reads, if only I had discovered them when I was eighteen my sex life could have been so much more interesting and inventive as some parts of the stories were very explicit indeed!

After a very wet and windy night I did all the usual chores which took quite a long time here as I was so far away from the amenities. There was a very elderly couple next door staying in a tiny tent which made Daisy seem really palatial especially in the wet weather. The poor souls looked really miserable and I would have offered to make them a cup of tea but when I smiled and was about to say something I was given 'the look' and so I didn't dare. I hadn't heard from the garage and so I decided to go and see what was happening and as I expected they were still waiting for the part. I took the decision to risk going off to explore the Llyn Peninsular and said I would be back around 3.30pm. I had an absolutely brilliant time. I drove to Abersoch and had a quick look around there which again was stunning and beautiful despite the rain. The mountains all around looked so dramatic with the low cloud smothering the tops, it was very atmospheric. I continued to the end of the peninsula to Aberdaron, wow! Just as I got there the sun came out. I parked in the NT car park and on a slope as the garage advised I could bump start her if the starter motor failed again. I visited the NT Visitor Centre which triggered within me a spiritual feel to the area and then I visited St. Hywyn's Church which is on a pilgrimage route and where the famous poet R.S. Thomas was vicar for some time.

It was an amazing place and I was very moved by what I saw and read in there. In fact it occurred to me for the first time that although it hadn't been in my thought process, it very much felt as though I was actually on a pilgrimage. How strange! Another extraordinary feature of this peninsular, is that it is at this point several strong currents in the sea converge which make it very dangerous for shipping and have been the cause of several shipwrecks in the past. I had an excellent lunch in the pub there and then drove back. I was blessed with seeing this extraordinarily beautiful and haunting area in rain and sun. A successful day as I got the starter motor fixed on my way back to the site and it was a sunny evening. I emailed my friend, Lindsay to ask what did she think the definition of 'pilgrimage' was and did she think that I could be on a pilgrimage in a campervan or did you have to be on foot?

You get to see all sorts on the sites and some aren't very pleasant. A family were staying not far from me and there was this really ignorant man, grossly overweight and absolutely horrible, shouting at his wife and daughter, a real bully, I felt so sorry for them. Equally you can get some lovely friendly people staying next to you which makes all the difference as to how you feel about the site.

Although going back on myself, I visited Harlech next and I'm glad I did, it was a lovely drive to it with gorgeous countryside, mountains and sea views. When I got to Harlech I realised I wasn't going to be able to make the tight turn into the town and so I went onto Llandanwg which is a delightful inlet with sand dunes and a medieval church. I parked Daisy and had a walk around the beautiful bay with the mountains acting as a dramatic backdrop to this beautiful area. Unfortunately, the little medieval church was closed but I did sit for a while beside it and to my delight there was a fly pass of Swifts, incredibly fast and very noisy.

I drove back to Harlech and was easily able to negotiate the turning onto the road from this angle which takes you up the hill into the town. Harlech is a Heritage Site, a town built up high on the top of the cliffs with its very impressive castle and, although a ruin, it is better than many I had come across. It has the most amazing views from all of its aspects, some looking out over the Irish Sea and others to the peaks of Snowdonia and inland. Its position would have made it an excellent fortification and its setting must be one of the most beautiful. Another feature of this castle is the defended 'Way from the Sea', a gated and fortified stairway plunging almost

200ft. down to the foot of the castle rock below and was used to provide access to supplies coming in from the sea. Now you have dunes between the castle and the sea but at one time the sea came right up to it. Harlech was built by Edward I when he invaded Wales, it was opened in 1283 and the architect was James of St. George. Interestingly, by the time it was fully operational in 1303, it had cost £8,184 (around 11million now) but it was still a third of the cost of Caernarfon or Conway. Harlech Castle played a key role in the national uprising led by Owain Glyndwr who did manage to take the castle and he used it as his headquarters for some time. Amazingly, Wales has 427 castles. By visiting the castles, you get to understand the history of Wales and the unrest which existed between England and Wales at the time. I'm so pleased we are all friends today.

I had a very enjoyable walk around the town. Although it is a little sad in places, it is still a very special place and I was really pleased I had made the decision to come back to visit it.

On my way back, I called at Portmeirion which I could see was quite special also but I didn't go in as it was expensive.

I felt that all of the places I had visited on the Llyn Peninsula were very spectacular, beautiful, spiritual and atmospheric. A fabulous area.

A near disaster on the oil level! It was time to pack up again and move onto Anglesey although I was sorry to leave this area. I hadn't gone far when I noticed a small garage attached to a shop and filling station and something told me to stop and get Daisy's oil level checked. Talk about divine intervention because when they checked her oil level it was dangerously low. If I had kept driving her I could have blown up the engine. She has to have special oil and it so happened there was a motor parts place just around the corner from them. I bought the oil and went back to the garage where the mechanics very kindly showed me how to pour more oil into her quickly by concocting a device made from a plastic bottle with the end chopped off and a piece of plastic pipe. Again, the mechanics didn't charge me for their help and time. This really renewed my faith in human nature and God, of course.

I drove to Llanberis where the train leaves for Snowdon. It was really busy when I got there with lots of people waiting for the train but fortunately I was able to get a ticket for the 3.30pm train. The Snowdon Mountain Railway describes itself as 'Taking you on the journey of a lifetime to the rooftop of Wales'. The trip up Snowdon was magical, another steam train journey and I felt quite smug as I watched the walkers struggling up the mountain. I was in carriage A with the guard and so I had a brilliant view. I was really lucky as it was a beautiful sunny day, the guard was telling me that a lot of the time the mountain is shrouded in mist or cloud and so you can't see that much. However, today was perfect, you could see for miles from the top plus it actually wasn't windy. It is described as having stunning scenery and awe-inspiring views from the top and that certainly isn't an exaggeration. It was breathtaking. There were lots of young people perilously climbing around on the rocks and having their photograph taken or doing 'selfies'. Jo's partner Lee phoned whilst I was at the top. The strangest experience ever to hear my phone ringing and then to be talking to someone so far away in that special place, so weird as he sounded so close. The train going up was a steam train but I had to catch the small diesel train coming back down but equally as thrilling. By the time I alighted the train back down at the station, I felt completely blown away by the whole experience. However, I had to come back down to earth as I had to complete the journey and I was going to be late reaching the next site on Anglesey. I rang the site to let them know that I would be late arriving.

You can tell how unprepared for this trip I was because I hadn't even realised that there were two bridges over the Menai Strait and of course I took the wrong one and ended up in Beaumaris. By the time I realised what had happened and found my way to the next site, I was really late. Fortunately, someone else was also late and so the proprietor had waited for us. The site was at Lligwy Bay right next to the beach. Fantastic! What a day, by the time I had found my spot on the site, I was so tired, I turned Daisy's interior into the bed and slept.

Up bright and early and time to explore again. I got Daisy ready and did a tour of the island and went across to Holyhead with a view to stopping at RSPB South Stack but it was absolutely heaving, the car parks were full and there were cars abandoned everywhere and so I just admired the beautiful scenery and carried on down the coast looking at the other beaches. They were a lot stonier and more rugged than the other side of the island and also a lot busier, I much preferred where I was staying. Content that I now had a good understanding of Anglesey, I relaxed and spent the rest of the day walking.

The site was perfectly positioned, it was a private site and so more expensive but worth every penny. It was a short walk to the beach where you could buy the most delicious bacon baps for breakfast and you were then on the coastal path. I walked the coastal path to Moelfre which has a small harbour and a pub. The views across to Llandudno made me speechless, wow! I had a pint of lager in the pub as it was really hot and it made a nice break before returning. As I was walking back the gulls were starting to come home to roost to the small island a little way off, what a racket they made. I sat and watched the Gannets fish for a while. What a spectacular sight! It is quite incredible the speed at which they hit the sea, head first. I read somewhere that they have developed special skulls which protect their brains as they enter the water and when you watch them you can appreciate why. When I got back I sat outside in the evening sunshine and watched the sun go down, the whole sky turned blood red, I have never seen anything like it.

What a strange day! Sunny and very hot. The previous evening, I thought I wouldn't bother to go to the local church as the English service was at 8.30am and there didn't seem much point going to the later service at 10am as it was in Welsh. However, I was up bright and early and so I thought I would make the effort. I left the site around 8am and got to the church in plenty of time. There were only four of us in church plus the priest, obviously the Welsh service was the more popular. I had all sorts of plans for what I was going to do afterwards but Daisy had a different idea and refused to start again. I sat in the church car park for over two hours waiting for the RAC to come out by which time people were arriving for the later service. I felt a right twit sat there and began to think that maybe Daisy was a folly of mine. At last Andy came to have a look at her. He tried everything but still couldn't get her going, and in the end, he bump started her and I had to drive back to the campsite with him following as there weren't any garages open. It was left that he would come back the next morning and help me to get to a garage. He was pretty certain that it was the starter motor again.

It was a fabulous day and so I broke out into shorts (which doesn't happen very often) and went down to the beach. I felt I was in a most gorgeous place and should make the most of the moment and not worry about tomorrow.

Tomorrow did come though and I had to sort things out. A stinking hot day, it would have been lovely to go back to the beach. I found out where the garage was but Andy had been sent on another breakdown some way off and wouldn't be able to help me and so I was left in the lurch. Eventually the garage owner came and towed Daisy to get her going and then we went to the garage. They gave me a courtesy car and told me to return around 4pm.

I found a beach close by which had a restaurant and so I had lunch there and a walk along the beach. I got back to the garage and they explained that it was the starter motor again and they would have to order a new part which wouldn't be there until the next day (a familiar story) and they couldn't get it going again and so it would have to stay with them. I had taken out special cover with the RAC designed for just this situation whereby if your van breaks down they will pay for a hotel as of course you have nowhere to sleep. I spent a very frustrating hour trying to sort things out over the phone with them. I explained the situation and they had a record of Andy's call out yesterday but rather than allow me to have an overnight stay in a hotel they wanted to tow me back to Cornwall. I explained that I was on a road trip, away from home for six months and I didn't want to go back home and Daisy was in a garage awaiting a part for the repair. Eventually, the young lady I was speaking to went and got her supervisor and again I explained the situation and that Andy was supposed to have come back to me this morning but didn't, but I had managed to get Daisy to the garage where she should be fixed the following day. She confirmed that all they could do was to take me back to Cornwall. By this time, I had lost the will to argue and went and found a hotel which I paid for but I did feel what was the point of the highly expensive RAC cover. If I had broken down during a weekday I would have been taken straight to a garage. I think I was a bit unlucky as I had already paid for a new starter motor and the fitting of it and now I faced another very large bill as it included the towing fee as well. I rang the garage where they fitted the other starter motor and said that if I took the starter motor back to them, I should be reimbursed for it. This meant that I would have to return to Pwllheli. At this point I just thought I really don't want to go back and so I will have to accept it, such is life! However, this on top of the money I had had to pay to have the caravan repaired, plus a hotel bill, meant that I had used up quite a large chunk of my funding for the trip.

It was a treat to sleep in a proper bed though and to have breakfast cooked for me. I contacted the garage to confirm that I could keep the courtesy car until Daisy was sorted.

Becky, my daughter-in-law, had arrranged for me to stay that evening with her dad, John and his wife, Lisel in Llandudno. I had to ring them to apologise as I would be arriving much later than intended.

Always look on the bright side of life, at least it gave me an opportunity to see a bit more of Anglesey. I drove to Beaumaris which was just as lovely as I remembered from that first evening. I booked a boat ride to Puffin Island. The boat ride was great as there was a nice breeze coming off the sea and very good value. We were out for about an hour touring around the island and there was a commentator telling you about the island and pointing out places of interest all of the way. The island was covered in nesting birds of many varieties including various types of gull and Guillemots. Puffins were nesting but you couldn't see them as they nest in the grass. However, we saw four flying off the island and two in the water but they were a little way off and so I'm not sure it counted as a proper sighting. We did see Seals and a Porpoise jumping out of the water, such an amazing sight. I didn't go into the castle when I got back but I explored the area all around. A lovely place!

It was 5pm by the time the garage called to say Daisy was ready. The starter motor they fitted in Pwllheli was too small which was why it had failed.

I had a wonderful evening ride to Llandudno. I loved going through the tunnel and driving around the outside of the walls of Conway Castle which I had planned to visit if everything had gone according to plan but it was too late now. It looked as though I missed a real treat. John and Lisel's welcome more than made up for the hassle of the last few days and I could look forward to another couple of nights sleeping on a proper bed.

Sometimes I was very surprised by places and this was one of them. I had a preconceived idea of how Llandudno would look which was totally wrong. It's beautiful. Lisel had to spend the day helping her 95-year-old father and so John took me for a walk around Great Orme, about five miles and quite steep in places. You can take a train or bus but I'm so glad we walked as I don't think I would have felt the proper majesty of this place otherwise. The rock formation is layered as on Anglesey. It was interesting to be looking over to Anglesey rather than the other way around. Afterwards we caught the bus to Rhos on Sea to meet Lisel and so I got to see a bit more of the area. Later when the sun was setting we went up onto the cliffs not far from where they live and watched the sunset which was blood red again, magical.

It was still very hot and so Lisel suggested we go off early the next day to visit Bodnant Gardens. Hidcote has always been my benchmark but these gardens had everything. There were rose gardens, three different ponds, boat houses, a mausoleum, a beautiful tree lined walk (some of the trees were planted in the 1700's) a mill, and waterfalls etc. It took us about four hours to walk around them. Some of the paths had been shut off because they were filming a

Secret Garden there, a perfect place to do that. After we left Lisel took me for a drive around to see some of the local beauty spots, some of the scenery was breathtaking.

We stopped at the Snowdon Electric Surf place, how peculiar to find a huge surf machine in the middle of mountains. It created perfect waves and so the surfers didn't have to hang around for ages as in the seas around Cornwall.

Before leaving the next day, John suggested we walk to Rhos along the seafront. We walked for a couple of miles and stopped and had coffee on the promenade. Prior to this we stopped and visited the smallest church on the British Isles, it was a tiny stone building on a site where a saint had previously built a church out of mud. It only housed five people and did feel very spiritual. Apparently, they still have a service in there every Thursday. We caught the bus into Llandudno and had lunch in an art gallery before returning to their house. When we got back I left virtually straight away having had an amazing couple of days. I was about to leave Wales.

I had spent six weeks in total in Wales which was a lot longer than I had anticipated. I realise that I have used words like 'beautiful' 'amazing' 'fantastic' 'stunning' 'breathtaking' 'spiritual' on numerous occasions. What can I say except that it was a very special place. The scenery is breathtaking and it is a very spiritual area, God's Country indeed. The weather wasn't always kind to me and trying to sort out Daisy's problems wasn't easy either but I had enjoyed the journey immensely and I had learnt so much.

Time to leave!

I would like to share with you this poem which I found in St. Hywyns Church, Aberdaron.

A poem by RS Thomas
'But the silence in the mind'
But the silence in the mind
is when we live best, within
listening distance of the silence
we call God. This is the deep
calling to deep of the psalm-
writer, the bottomless ocean
we launch an armada of
our thought on, never arriving.

It is a presence, then,
whose margins are our margins;
that calls us out over our
own fathoms. What to do
but draw a little nearer to
such ubiquity by remaining still?

A growing sense of Pilgrimage

Beautiful Snowdonia

Lligwy

The walk to Moelfre

Bodnant Gardens

Chapter 6

An aside

As I mentioned before, I had been away for over six weeks and I had developed a rhythm of living very simply. Daisy had caused me a few problems but I had overcome them. I guess she is basically a tin box and so can be very cold and equally very hot but she has a lot of windows and so light and airy and her cheerful interior is always very welcoming. The sound of rain on the roof can be a bit alarming but I was getting used to most of her foibles. I liked the pace of life she offered and I could park her easily in most spaces.

By this time, I was starting to feel pretty fit from all the walking I was doing and as I was tired most nights I was sleeping so much better. The healthy eating helped as well, I had lost weight. I didn't attempt fancy meals but bought fresh fish whenever I could, I ate a lot of salads and omelettes and then had the odd treat at a restaurant or I bought fish and chips occasionally. One of the good things about the CCC sites was that most Fridays wherever you were, a fish and chip van would come around. Also, I was very tanned from all the outdoor activities and being by the sea. I was alone but I could enjoy watching families and couples having fun together again without feeling like Mrs. No Friends.

As well as feeling physically so much better, I felt very much that I was on a spiritual journey. Most days I was experiencing new and different places each having its own special charm and beauty. I had visited many amazing places of worship from small to large and I was starting to make a connection with something beyond everyday life. My prayers were no longer just for family and friends but were channelled much more towards praying for peace in the world and for the hundreds of refugees.

I have felt very blessed to have been born into this country which is by no means perfect, and we have experienced a very bloody history, but we are no longer torn by war and as a democracy we have a lot of freedoms. I was born not that long after the Second World War and so it was still a regular topic of conversation within families then, most of whom had lost someone to the war and for those who had returned safely home, life was often never the same again. Also, there was still food rationing although I can never remember feeling hungry. I can only imagine from what I see on the news what it must be like to be caught up in a war such as is raging in Syria and Ukraine. It must be terrifying, having your home taken from you and having to seek life somewhere else whilst trying to protect your family.

Some years ago, I read E.V. Morton's book 'In the steps of the Master'. He was a travel writer in the 1930's and this book was about his journey following in Christ's footsteps through Palestine and Trans-Jordan. I think he would be horrified to see what has happened in recent years especially in Syria, that poor country and its divided people, civil war must surely be of the worst kind. At the time he wrote the book people of all faiths were living in harmony with one another. I remember his description of Aleppo, of its beauty and its people. It is heartbreaking to see it so battered by warfare.

What I find interesting is the way the world has split almost into two factions. On the one hand you have peoples who are returning to a more tribal mode of living such as in Afghanistan and parts of Africa and then you have the juxtaposition of others sending probes into outer space to discover the universe. How extraordinary!

Chapter 7

Chester, Liverpool, The Peak District and Lancashire
June 30th – July 13th

July so far had been really hot and although Daisy's cool box worked well most of the time, I had inadvertently switched it off and so I had to throw everything away and start again. This meant a stop at Tesco's on the way to Delamere Forest. I tried to avoid supermarkets but sometimes needs must. I arrived at the site around 6.30pm and it was still really hot.

Even though I was staying on a site in a forest which was lovely and there were lots of trees dotted about, I had very little shade where I was until midday. Daisy was already boiling hot by 7am. I was planning to do a walk but the heat and inertia hit me and so I attached my home-made sun shade to the side of Daisy (whilst a complete and utter failure in windy Wales it was perfect here as not even a breeze to blow it off) and I gave myself the day off. It was time to break out into shorts and T shirt and just sit. For the first time during the trip I got out my sketch pad and drew the tree just in front of me. I can't draw to save my life but it was very therapeutic and as I wasn't planning on anyone else seeing it, it didn't matter. The day just disappeared in a haze of heat and drinks. It was fun watching the children in the field playing with water pistols screeching with joy every time they got a drenching.

I was up early the next morning as I had planned to catch the train into Chester to go to Evensong in Chester Cathedral but when I got to the station there was a notice saying 'no train that day due to engineering works but a bus service would pick up at the telephone box'. There was another couple waiting by the telephone box (they were staying on the same site as me), they were going to Liverpool to meet friends. They made me laugh, they had spent most of the night at the hospital as she had fallen over whilst jiving having partaken of too much wine and fractured a bone in her wrist. Poor her but at least she could laugh about it. We stood there like lemons waiting for the bus which never materialised. They got a taxi but I gave up as I was meeting Becky's mum in Chester in a few days' time. Instead I did a lovely walk around the lakes which weren't far from the site, it was mostly in the shade. One of the lakes looked almost like a swamp, it had lots of what looked like broken off tree trunks sticking out of the water. I was surprised to come across a group of people looking very dirty and sweaty crawling under nets and jumping over obstacles, I found out later they were doing a type of outward bound course for charity, rather them than me on such a hot day.

I was a lot more successful the following day and I did manage to catch the train into Liverpool having changed at Chester. I made straight for the cathedral which was very well sign posted and so easy to find. I was blown away by it, supposedly Britain's largest cathedral. It is quite a forbidding structure as built from a dark red stone but other than that I thought it was beautiful, vast. There was a school choir in there practising for a performance and so I sat and listened for a while. They continued as I looked around and so a lovely backdrop to my wanderings. I spent a long time looking at all the glorious areas, the Baptistry and the stunning Great West Window. There was a Communion Service just about to take place in the Lady Chapel and so I joined in, it kind of made up for missing Evensong yesterday. My visit ended with the lighting of a candle and prayers.

I had planned on visiting the Catholic cathedral as well but I had spent too long in the other cathedral and I wanted to visit the Terracotta Army exhibition in the World Museum and so, unfortunately, I didn't have time.

I was very surprised by the cultural centre of Liverpool. In my ignorance I always associate Liverpool with the pop era and the

Beatles or its docks and shipping. In fact, it has a fine centre with some beautiful buildings, the World Museum being one of them. I spent a long time looking at the Terracotta Army exhibition as it was so interesting. There were only five of the warriors there but even so they were very impressive. The life size statues were beautifully carved and each one different and I realized why after reading the information boards, they were all based on actual individuals. There were also two chariots on display, again very finely carved and very true to life. I can only imagine what it must be like to visit the whole army in China, maybe one day I will. In the meantime, I had at least had a very good introduction to how the way of life in China was at that time and its traditions. Amazing, so interesting.

I negotiated my way back to the station and thought about the wonders I had just seen. It was awe inspiring to think about the amount of skill and effort which must have gone into creating the army. I somehow managed to get back to the site safely and felt very grown up having negotiated the day on my own. It had been another really hot day and so I was very tired when I got back.

I finally made it to Chester where I met up with Ann, Becky's mum. It was great to see a friendly face and we had a lovely day. She showed me all around, we walked the city walls which were made from a red sandstone and then down by the river where we had a splendid lunch. We had a look at the original cathedral, St. John's, which is now a church, a fascinating journey back through time to AD689 when the church was founded. It was given the status of 'Cathedral' in 1075 but after the Reformation it fell into disrepair. Elizabeth I then granted it St. John's Parish Church Status. Not only does it have a very interesting history but also its architecture is remarkable, 'a fine example of the transition from the heavy Norman/Romanesque of the Nave pillars to the slender Gothic of the Triforium and Clerestory'. If Ann hadn't taken me there I would probably have gone straight to the present day cathedral but it was well worth the visit.

We did then go on to visit Chester Cathedral which stands on the site of a 10th Century Saxon Church, another amazing building with an interesting history. It is built out of a lighter reddish stone to Liverpool. The choir were practising for the evening performance of the Mystery Plays, beautiful haunting music. I loved the centre of Chester with its Tudor half-timber buildings and little alleyways going off, it reminded me a bit of York. The Town Crier was in the centre drawing in the tourists with his amusing comments, he was especially targeting some young Spanish girls who were obviously enjoying the attention. Thanks to Ann I had a really good day.

Next stop, Leek! Before leaving I thought I would give Daisy a good clean up. I have mentioned previously that I was living very basically but I did have some emergency toilet provision in Daisy. I had a square box with a padded lid to sit on and inside, a bucket with a lid. It did the job. However, on this occasion after emptying it in the special place, I had forgotten to pick it up and went off to brush my teeth. It was some considerable time later that I realised what I had done and although empty I would have hated for anyone to look inside as I hadn't cleaned it and so probably pretty smelly. How embarrassing if someone had handed it into reception and I had to go and collect it. I felt a bit like Inspector Clouseau as I made a stealthy approach back to make sure no one was around and thankfully it was still there and I was able to retrieve it without anyone seeing. Phew!

My trip to Leek was fairly uneventful. Since working out my routes by map instead of relying solely on the SATNAV I wasn't getting lost quite so often and thankfully on this site I had a pitch under a tree providing much needed shade which was wonderful.

The following day I decided to be quite adventurous. I could see from the map book and the little arrows on the contours that there were steep ups and downs on the route but I really wanted to visit Chatsworth House and Bakewell, home of the tarts. I was crossing over from Staffordshire into Derbyshire. It should have been about an hour's journey but the route took me on lanes and B roads which went up and down. As it happens Daisy coped very well. At one point she had to contend with a 40% rise on the way there and of course down on the way back, the road had many double bends and the odd hairpin bend and despite her oil temperature going to maximum level she coped really well with the challenge, I was very proud of her.

We went across the main Buxton road and the scenery was stunning. We passed small pretty villages and the views when high up were absolutely breathtaking, rocky outcrops surrounded by purple heather with armies of Foxgloves standing guard over the whole scene. I eventually arrived at Chatsworth House. Wow! What a pile, more like a palace than a stately home. It was fairly expensive to go in but worth every penny. It is hard to put into words the splendour of this house, anyone who has been to see it will understand what I mean, you really do just have to see it. I spent a long time wandering around as it is vast and so much to see, not only the rooms which are splendid in themselves but the collections of porcelain and all sorts of different artefacts from all over the world, some of it very old and some modern, a wonderful eclectic mix. The paintings are amazing as well. Most aspects of the house I loved but there were parts I felt too ostentatious and overbearing for my taste. There is a room done out in oak panelling with lots of carvings which I thought really over the top and in another of the rooms all the walls were covered in patterned leather. I have never seen anything like it before and it must have cost a fortune.

I was mesmerised in particular by the Veiled Vestal Virgin by Rafaelle Monti, a statue of a beautiful and graceful young woman kneeling, she has a crown of flowers around her head, with a veil which drapes around her head and body over very simple clothing. Her arms are outstretched holding a plate with an offering on it. At first, I thought she was a young bride. I'm not an expert and so I have no idea what she is made of but it looked to me as though she is carved out of very fine white alabaster or pure marble. I just can't imagine how Rafaelle Monti who created the sculpture managed to get the fineness of the veil in which she is swathed to look so real, her features and expression are just beautiful. Every now and then I see a piece of artwork which seems to me to be so exquisite that it brings tears to my eyes and this was one of those occasions. I found it to be breathtaking, it was as though she could come to life at any moment. It was surrounded by glass to stop you getting too close and so it must be extremely valuable and very well loved by the owners. I would have loved to find out more about it.

I eventually left the inside of the house to explore the outside which is just as palatial with window surrounds of presumably gold leaf paint and even the pineapples on top of the roof were gold. You couldn't have a house of this stature without gardens to delight and they did not disappoint. I spent a long time exploring them and soaking up their beauty. A wonderful day spent enthralled by history and beauty. I can't imagine the cost and effort required to keep this 'treasure' to such a high standard for us all to be able to enjoy. A huge 'thankyou' to Lord and Lady Chatsworth and to their army of staff for allowing me to have had this experience albeit at a cost, but I was pleased to contribute.

Afterwards I did drive to Bakewell, a very pretty town built by a river. I parked Daisy and had a very enjoyable stroll around, a perfect end to a perfect day.

Every now and again you are reminded of the dangers of driving. The following day I waited for a bus outside the site to go into Leek which didn't turn up and so I tried for a later one, again it didn't turn up. I found out afterwards that there had been a serious accident just outside Buxton causing the road to be closed for some time. A few days ago, I was talking to a guy who arrived at the Delamere site late because he was at the scene of another horrible accident where people were seriously hurt. I rang my grandson, Michael yesterday to wish him a Happy Birthday and he was telling me of a dreadful accident back home. Oh dear! I touched my St. Christopher which as promised I hadn't taken off since I'd been away.

Ann and Pete were joining me at Leek and so I went off into Leek early to buy some bits and pieces for lunch. I found an Aldi with a huge car park, perfect. It wasn't open as it was a Sunday and so I was too early. I left Daisy there and went into Leek to have a look around, a pretty town. I thought I would just visit a church but the next thing I am taking part in a Communion Service at St. Luke's.

It was rather nice and I stayed and had a cup of coffee and chat afterwards. I was quite some time but I didn't think anything about it. I went back to Aldi and bought cold meats, pate, crusty bread and salad plus a couple of really nice bottles of wine. I also treated myself to croissants. A few weeks later I received a parking fine from Aldi! Oops! They did drop the fine once I explained what I had done and produced evidence of my purchases. They have a camera which registers when you go in and out. However, I was oblivious to this on the day.

I drove back to the site and brewed a pot of coffee in my Italian device, one of those luxuries I bought before I left. This with a croissant made me feel as though I had died and gone to heaven. Ann and Pete were late arriving as Ann had hurt her knee and they had called at A & E but as they didn't find anything wrong, they continued with their journey. The weather was still fabulous and so we were able to eat lunch outside. Ann was obviously in discomfort and so I offered her some of my strong painkillers before walking the 0.5 miles to the pub in the evening. She really frightened Pete and me as we were sitting in the pub waiting for our food to arrive, and then suddenly Ann keeled over on to the seat. I thought the worst but as it turned out she had fallen asleep, the painkillers I had provided her with were obviously too strong for her, she is quite tiny. I felt really bad. We got a taxi back. She was fine and we sat outside as it was such a beautiful evening, the sky full of stars, I loved these evenings.

The temperature had reached 30 degrees but the following day it started to get cooler again. After breakfast Ann and Pete left the site on their way to island hop around Scotland. We agreed to meet up again at Culzean Castle in a month's time. It was time for me to move on as well after booking the next stopping off points. I was surprised that I managed to get a booking at Culzean Castle so easily and then the staff told me that it was the worst time for midges there and gave me all sorts of tips on how to cope with them. It didn't fill me with a longing to go there.

The Peak district really is beautiful but can be quite challenging whilst driving an old VW and I knew I was in for an interesting drive to Crowden. The drive between Leek and Buxton was steep but fine and the scenery amazing. The rocky hills which are almost mountains on either side of the road were bathed in sunshine with huge stones jutting out and with swathes of the pink Rosebay Willowherb and purple heather. Glorious. I was going to stop at Buxton which looked interesting, I would have liked to visit Poole's Cavern but decided today would be all about the scenery. The one thing I didn't want to do was to find myself on the B6105 just past Glossop and what happened? I found myself on the B6105. I had seen from the contours on the map book that there were some really steep ups and downs on this road leading across the top of the Peaks. At one point I put Daisy into second gear from third too early coming down a really steep hill and she objected by making a scary popping sound and then there was a burning smell. I held my breath because I wasn't sure what was going to happen but she kept going and everything seemed to be working, particularly the brakes and gears, thank God. The worst bit was at the end though when I had to make a really sharp left turn onto a very busy main road. Wow! Talk about terrifying. At last a kind person stopped to let me out but I had to take in the other lane as well, I just prayed nothing would come around the bend. I somehow made it to the next site in one piece. The drive had had its scary moments but worth it to experience the absolutely stunning scenery.

Having reached Crowden, I just sat for a while with a well-earned cup of tea trying to come back down to earth. I got chatting to a couple from the Isles of Scilly and they asked my advice about getting to Cornwall and what to see when they got there. With my new-found map reading skills and after all of the places I had visited, I was able to give it. I also got chatting to a guy next door who was from S. Ireland. He made me smile because he had decided to have a major laundry day and was walking around in some very sexy skimpy swimmers, they didn't leave a lot to the imagination.

I was starting to relax. I went for a walk up the hill from the site as I wanted to get a telephone signal and when I got back a lovely lady brought me a piece of her birthday cake. I thought that it was such a kind thing to do.

I absolutely love Thai food and so the following day, despite the heat, I decided to walk into Hadfield from the site which should have been a ten-mile round trip. The warden gave me directions and said, "You can't possibly go wrong." Famous last words! I followed the Pennine Way for a while and then across the bridge which ran over the Reservoir. All was going according to plan until the next bridge over the dam where it wasn't clear what to do. I thought I had to go straight on but this led me to the dreaded B6105 and so I had to backtrack. Fortunately, I found someone to ask. The path I wanted was a disused railway track that led straight into Hadfield, it was a lovely walk. I have to say I was somewhat disappointed with Hadfield. In fact I walked down a street and asked where the main High Street was and apparently I had just walked down it. I eventually found the Thai restaurant hoping to have lunch there but it didn't open until 4pm and it was only 1pm. There was no way I could spend three hours in Hadfield and so I bought a wrap from a Tesco Express and ate it on the way back. How disappointing!

The journey from hell! After talking to one of the wardens on the site, I decided to change my route to Clitheroe and go the shorter way rather than the longer scenic route. What a mistake! The idea was to skirt Manchester on the A road. The route was carefully planned and all went fine until I couldn't find the sign to see which lane I needed because it was hidden behind trees. By the time I spotted it, it was too late and I got in a right mess as I didn't know where to go. A huge lorry had snuck up behind me and beeped extremely loudly when I signalled to change into his lane. Thankgoodness he did. However, this forced me to go onto the M60 ring road around Manchester and various other places. Ugh! I have always thought I would hate the M25 but this motorway took the biscuit. There were no slip roads, just lanes going off and as Daisy isn't the fastest vehicle on the road, I was often in the wrong lane and so had to swap lanes quite frequently. I have to say the drivers around there were maniacs and not very giving, they showed no mercy whatsoever. Talk about risking life and limb. At one point I had to come off and go onto the M66 and whilst changing motorways a car came from nowhere doing over 100 miles per hour. I couldn't believe it, somehow, he managed to miss me. If I'd been in a car going that bit faster, he would have hit me. If I had had time to see his number plate, I would have reported him but he had disappeared in an instant. The idiot! I managed to keep my head and eventually reached Padiham where I wanted to visit a stately home. Gawthorpe Hall is a beautiful Elizabethan country house built on the banks of the River Calder. It was the sort of house you could imagine yourself living in as it was not ostentatious and the rooms were beautiful. I also loved the gardens especially the, typical of its day, box hedged garden.

I was using the SATNAV again to find my way around but trying to find the next site was really difficult and so I resorted to my phone and google maps which I was finding far more reliable. The site in Clitheroe was by a river, really beautiful. By the time I got there I was exhausted and so I went and sat by it for a long time to relax. After such a really awful journey, I was feeling pretty shook up. I now know why I hate driving. This was by far the most stressful day of driving yet and as I felt my St. Christopher, which hadn't left me for a moment, I felt very glad to be alive. I had decided not to mention any of this to friends and family.

I had a rest from driving the next day and walked into Clitheroe town. I stopped off at St. Luke's Church and gave a prayer of thanksgiving for keeping me safe yesterday. I really liked Clitheroe town. It was very jolly with all the bunting up and it had some really nice shops plus a castle which although a ruin, is still quite imposing as it is situated on the top of a hill overlooking the town. I had a coffee in the Old Emporium which had been beautifully done out with chandeliers and huge pot plants, a bit Victorian and the seating was on various levels, it served good coffee too. I tried a number of hairdressers to see if they had a free slot as my hair was starting to look really dreadful and in need of TLC but everywhere was fully booked. I would just have to start wearing it up. I walked back and spent the afternoon sat by the river reading, plus I did some research as to where to spend my birthday, I thought I would treat myself to a night in a hotel. I decided on Thornham Hall just outside Lancaster.

This would make for a rather strange episode in my journey but I hadn't appreciated this at the time.

The end of another chapter in my journey and I was still alive to tell the tale!

My homemade shade worked

Liverpool Cathderal
(my photo doesn't do it justice)

Two of the Terracotta Warriors

The Veiled Vestal Virgin
At Chatsworth House

Chapter 8

Cumbria, the Lake district and Northumberland
July 13th – August 1st

By now the weather had started to change, it had rained for a while and had become very humid. After the last horrendous drive I was very apprehensive about driving again and the fluttering anxious tummy had returned albeit briefly, but I was free again and heading through the Yorkshire Dales National Park to Kendal. Although it was a longer route it meant I was able to avoid the M6 and it was very pretty. Apart from being slightly thrown at one point by queues of traffic heading for a festival and another near miss when a lorry decided to overtake a dustcart and I had to slam the brakes on, the drive was fairly uneventful and was stunning, such a pretty part of the country; my trip today was all about scenery again. Why didn't I keep to my original plan when leaving Crowden? Lesson learnt! The site at Kendal was yet another CCC site and again situated by a beautiful river. After getting organised I walked along the River Mint into Kendal, a really peaceful walk, lots of beautiful wildflowers everywhere. By the time I reached Kendal the shops were closing but I did find a shop which sold the famous Kendal Mint Cake. The evening walk back was equally wonderful, the air was full of the heady scent of the wildflowers and grasses.

The next day I got talking to this lovely lady who was also from Cornwall. She was with her 'other half' who she told me was just a bit older than her son and twenty years younger than herself (I thought he was her son). They had such a romantic story to tell. Even though he was so much younger than her, one day he said that he wanted her to have his baby and despite her having turned forty they had a daughter. How wonderful! They seemed really happy together. He was quite dishy and so I thought there was hope for me yet. She was so funny, she really made me laugh.

I was on this site for only one night as I had booked a place on a site near Windermere which wasn't far away. I negotiated staying until 1pm and then I set off for Windermere but before leaving I finished planning the next leg of my journey which would take me up to the end of August.

The Windermere site was quite large but split into sections with lots of beautiful trees and so very private. There were a number of rabbits hopping around and some very friendly birds which included a pair of Pheasants looking for tit bits.

I had thought the weather would change but much to my surprise the sun shone again although a little cooler than it had been, thankgoodness. It was a Sunday and my plan was to skip going to find a church (something always seemed to go wrong) and head straight to Lake Windermere. However, the Lord had other plans for me and as I approached a church on the way through Windermere, people were just going in and so on the spur of the moment I found myself signalling to go into the car park. What a lovely church St Mary's is! One of the Church Wardens chatted to me for some time and told me that the church had been modernised after a fire had destroyed the roof. It had certainly been very tastefully done. In fact, it was palatial with carpet and very comfortable armchairs and a glass partitioned area for meetings etc. Very different to the Victorian concept of the hard pews. I hadn't experienced such 'High Church' in a long time, the priest and two officiates paraded in followed by the choir. I'm sure there aren't many churches that can boast of having such a significant number of people in their choir, it made a lot of difference to the singing. It was a Holy Communion Service and they even had bells although no smells. I was delighted to have found the church as they were so friendly. I didn't stay for coffee as I knew I had a busy day ahead of me.

I found my way through Windermere and Burness to the lake. Oh my goodness! both towns were so busy with foreign tourists, they were heaving. I eventually found somewhere to park on the long stay car park where I was able to buy a ticket for a tour of the lake and there was a small train which takes you to the quay from where you catch the boat. When we reached the quay there were so many coaches parked alongside with so many people emerging from them. I got caught up in a group of Americans, Japanese and Indians. Oh my! We lived in Fowey for a time some years ago when we first lived in Cornwall and every now and again one of the huge passenger liners would come into the harbour and then the town and surrounding area would be completely taken over by tourists as they emerged from this enormous hotel on the sea but that was nothing compared to this, it was unbelievable. I was swept along in the throng of people. Once I was on the boat, which I think held over 500 passengers, it was fine. The scenery was out of this world and the boat was the perfect place to see it from. The blue of the lake was complimented by the blue of the sky with stunning scenery everywhere you looked. I loved it and it was worth the hassle prior to boarding. I did the ride to Ambleside and back which took a couple of hours. What an amazing experience!

I walked to Burness to have a wander around the town but I couldn't cope with the huge numbers of people milling about and so I made my way back to Daisy and then drove to the site. It had been an unexpected and amazing day.

From Windermere I kind of went back on myself as I wanted to see Lancaster and the coastal area around it. On reflection I should probably have gone there from Clitheroe but then I would have missed out on the beautiful drive through the Dales and also it meant the timing was perfect for staying in a hotel for my birthday.

On the way to Lancaster I stopped off at Sizergh Castle (not far from Kendal) and arrived just in time for a tour which was really interesting. The Strickland family have lived there for hundreds of years. They were Catholics and so there were many fall outs with Henry and the family was in disgrace for quite a while but they managed to survive. There were family portraits everywhere, how incredible to belong to such a family. The main feature for me was the Tudor panelling everywhere and the lavishly carved overmantels plus the beautiful old floorboards which only hundreds of years of being exposed to polish and wear can create that certain patina. I also loved the vegetable and cut flower garden, you can imagine very little has changed over the years when they would have been very self-sufficient. The National Trust looks after the house etc. now but the family still live in part of it and it is closed to the public for special family occasions.

On leaving the castle I eventually found the A5105, the coastal road which takes you past Morecombe and Heysham. I had a bit of a wander around and then found my way to Lancaster. Driving through Lancaster wasn't very easy as it was so busy. It was around 4pm and so I guess there was a lot of school traffic but I managed to find my way through to Thurnham Hall. The hotel was everything I had hoped for. Thurnham Hall itself was very impressive but I was staying in a studio apartment in a block in the grounds, presumably an old stable block. It had a large area with a king size bed and seating plus TV, a kitchenette with a huge fridge and everything you could possibly need in a kitchen and then a huge bathroom with a corner bath and shower over it. I felt very spoilt to have all of this to myself. Can you imagine what it is like to relax in a beautiful hot bath in your own bathroom when for so long I had been sharing shower blocks with a multitude of other people? There was a TV, what luxury. I caught up on the news and then bliss, there was Monty and his gardening programme. Bedtime was incredible as I slipped under the covers and sank into the huge soft bed, I thought I had died and gone to heaven.

I don't care how old I become I just love a birthday, I still get very excited. Last year I decided to take ten years off my age as I don't feel old and as long as you don't look in the mirror it's fine. It was a lovely sunny warm day which started with lots of birthday messages from family and friends followed by another foamy hot bath (I thought I should make the most of it) I stayed in for so long my fingers became wrinkled. The hotel had leisure facilities and so I could have stayed around the hotel but I really wanted to see Lancaster. However, I did have a wander around the grounds first and sat by the lake watching the antics of the many ducks some of which were on the lake and some waddling around looking for food or having a clean-up. Having booked to have an evening meal in the dining room of the Hall, I ordered a taxi to take me into Lancaster (another treat, no driving). I spent a fascinating day!

Firstly, I visited St. Peter's Cathedral, a Catholic cathedral built in the shape of a cross, consecrated in 1859. Interestingly The Lady Chapel was donated by the Dalton family who then lived at Thurnham Hall. It has lovely stained glass windows, a beautiful Rose window inspired by Dante's Il Paradiso and the English Martyrs' window. At the bottom is Henry VIII who ordered the executions of Fisher and Moore two of the martyrs depicted in the window. Behind the iron screen at the back of the Sanctuary is the Blessed Sacrament Chapel a special place of prayer, the altar is made of white marble with an image of the last supper. Stunning. I found the Triptych which is made up of 32 panels depicting the scenes of the Passion which was very moving. The cathedral isn't huge but there are so many beautiful and interesting things to look at and it has a very spiritual atmosphere. I lit a candle and prayed for Richard and his mother who were both Catholics; Richard was a somewhat lapsed one and his mother stopped going to church when they stopped having the Latin Mass.

I visited Lancaster's museum which was brilliant for finding out about the history of Lancaster and the surrounding areas and I got a real feel for what it would have been like to live through the War of the Roses. The exhibition on the lower floor was centred on witchcraft based around the Pendle Witches, an awful time in history when some poor souls were found guilty of witchcraft based only on hearsay and rumour, it was really barbaric. They were tried at the castle prison and most of them were sentenced to death by hanging. There was also a section showing where JK Rowling got her stories from for her Harry Potter books.

I had the perfect birthday lunch in The Merchants Pub which was just down from the castle - melon and mozzarella cheese tart with basil and tomato, mouth wateringly good.

After lunch I walked up to the castle which is a very imposing building built on the site of an old Roman Fort overlooking Lancaster and which was still being used as a prison up until about ten years ago. I did the guided tour which took you around the old part of the castle where the dungeons are and where the 'instruments' were kept (really gruesome) and then into the Criminal and Civil Courtrooms still used today. It was supposed to be one of the 'better' prisons but I really don't know how people survived being incarcerated in there. It must have been dreadful if you were waiting to be transported or even worse to be taken to the Hanging Corner to be executed. Other than being famous for the Pendle Witches trial, during the First World War when German people living in this country were incarcerated, Joseph Pilates was interned there and it is said that he further developed the Pilates exercises to stay fit and which are still used today. You can't help but feel a darkness there, all of that human misery and although the whole place gave me the creeps I can't deny it was a really fascinating place to visit.

I would have liked to have done the Lune Aqueduct Experience on the canal but I ran out of time and so I caught a taxi back to the hotel. When I arrived back at the apartment the staff had left me a bottle of wine and some chocolates (I think I may have mentioned more than once that it was my birthday). How brilliant of them, it was a very unexpected and a lovely surprise.

I maybe hadn't mentioned but Daisy has a small wardrobe and so I was able to bring a 'posh frock' and heeled shoes with me. For the first time since being away I dressed up in my lacy black dress, make-up the lot and went to the Hall to dine. I felt like a million dollars as this was the first time in months that I wasn't wearing jeans. The dining room was very stylish and so was the food. I had Hake which tasted divine and a glass of an excellent white wine, it was just a shame I didn't have anyone to share the experience with. Apart from that I had had a fantastic birthday.

I made the most of the hotel facilities and had another bath before I left which I felt a bit bad about as they hadn't had any significant rainfall there since April and so water was in short supply. However, it was raining by the time I left and so I didn't feel quite so bad. I was heading for Ravenglass.

The plan was to join the M6 for a short distance to save going through Lancaster and then exit it and come off to join the A6 but I made a right mess of it and realised that I was heading for Blackpool which was in the wrong direction. I ended up having to travel ten miles to get off the motorway and then ten miles to get back on it and so twenty miles added on to my journey. At last I was following my planned route until suddenly I didn't seem to be on a main road and so I thought I must have missed the turn and so I did what the SATNAV said. Such a mistake, or was it? I had left the Yorkshire Dales and entered the Lake District National Park. I found myself in the middle of nowhere on a single track road going uphill and down dale sandwiched between mountains. At first, I was bewitched by the breathtaking scenery which was amazing even in the drizzle but then I became really frightened as I realised I didn't know where I was and if Daisy broke down, I knew I wouldn't be able to get a signal to phone for help, added to which I had been driving for miles and not seen a soul. At last I spotted a sign to Eskdale which I knew wasn't far from Ravenglass. It was a rusty long neglected in the middle of nowhere signpost but I decided to follow it come what may. It involved doing a very tricky manoeuvre around a steep hairpin bend but I was getting pretty good at doing this especially as I could be fairly assured that nothing would be coming the other way. Daisy was a star as she went up and down the steep hills and eventually we reached Eskdale. I was never so pleased to be back in civilisation. I had had a few very worrying moments but once safe I was so glad to have taken that route, it was quite something. I'll never forget the beauty which surrounded me.

I found myself under a tree on the next site and at first I found the continuous drip, drip onto Daisy's roof really annoying but after a while it became mesmerising and soothing and the rain was very refreshing after the long period of hot weather. I watched a Tree Creeper for a while but it then disappeared, really thrilling. I formulated a plan for my stay which involved a steam train ride and a visit to a castle plus some lovely walking.

I experienced my first encounter with the Romans and Hadrian's wall. Ravenglass was a major Roman Port in AD220 because of its natural harbour. The Roman Fort of Ravenglass was established in AD130 on the site of an earlier fortlet. The 'Bath House' walls here are amongst the tallest surviving remains along the Frontier. Apparently their occupation was a very peaceful affair no doubt because of the wealth they would have brought to the area.

I found this area to be very special.

I walked from the CCC site to the natural harbour which is really pretty, I lingered there to try and visualise what it would have looked like in Roman times. I could imagine it would have been bustling with the coming and going of ships and goods, Romans shouting out orders, I'm sure it would have been very noisy. In contrast, today all was peace and calm, a seemingly sleepy place.

Today I was excited as I had another steam train adventure to look forward to, I caught the train from Ravenglass up to Eskdale. I sat in one of the open carriages which was just a wooden box on wheels with no roof. Thankfully it had stopped raining and you got a great view from it as the train chugged on up the hill for about an hour through stunning scenery with the breeze blowing through your hair, great fun. Once at the top, there are a number of walks that you can do through protected woodland, all very well signposted. I went to discover Dalgeth Falls but because it had been so dry there wasn't a great deal of water flowing down but I could imagine they would be very spectacular after a period of heavy rainfall. As I had time I also did the walk to the church which was quite simple but lovely, beautiful stained glass windows. Outside there were lots of children playing on the stepping stones across the river. It looked as though a whole load of mums had organised a picnic there and they were having great fun. It reminded me of when my friend Conryn and I would take our children out for the day for a picnic by a river, such special times. The train up had a diesel engine but I caught the steam train back down and although it is a tiny engine you still get to feel as though you are going extremely fast. I can fully understand steam enthusiasts, there is just something about the noise and the smell and the steam, the whistle blowing that makes it such an exciting experience. What a great day!

Most of the wardens on the CCC sites are very helpful but there was a particularly lovely Scottish couple on this site who were so friendly which as I have said before is really important when you are on your own. When I mentioned I was driving to Muncaster Castle that day they told me of a route whereby you could walk there from the site following the Esk trail. It turned out to be a lovely walk past the ruins of the Roman Bath House and so I stopped to look. They are really amazing, to think they have stood for thousands of years. A number of the walls are still in place with windows and doors and so you get a very clear picture of how they would have looked. Incredible!

It took me about half an hour to get to Muncaster Castle which is a beautiful building surrounded by amazing views. It has a really interesting history, the castle dates from the medieval period and is situated looking out over the highest mountains in England, part of the Cumbrian Mountain range. It was built around 1208 by the Pennington family to guard the strategic point where the mountains meet the sea. Most of the 77 acres of grounds are natural but there is a half mile terraced garden which has a Yew Hedge around it, the views from here are stunning looking out over the mountains and the Himalayan Gardens. The family now are very hands on in running the castle as a business. I found here my dream library which was founded by the fifth Baronet. How to describe this stunning room in words? They could never do it justice. The room is circular with a very high domed ceiling painted in a dark blue with the star signs painted on it in gold. It has a gallery all around made from wood and brass and it contains bookshelves which go all the way to the floor housing thousands of books accessed by a movable ladder. There is a very homely and comfortable seating area around a beautiful fireplace and then huge windows at one end of the room overlooking the mountains, views to die for. If I lived in this house, I don't think I would ever be able to bring myself to leave that room. Having said that the rest of the house is gorgeous with amazing fireplaces, paintings and furniture. There is even a haunted room which doesn't surprise me. It feels like a home albeit a very grand one. The castle is closed on some Saturdays because it is used as a wedding venue and I can imagine what a great place it would be to get married in.

I had hoped to go to a service in St. Mary's Church on the estate but I forgot it was a fifth Sunday and so no service that day which was a bit disappointing. However, it did mean that I was able to see the owl display, the best I have ever seen, and the stars of the show were undoubtedly Lynton and Christie, two tiny Burrowing Owls that could run really fast, they were so cute. In the afternoon there was another amazing display in the grounds with hawks, vultures and eagles. The stars of this show for me were the Yellow Beaked Eagles. There were four of them weaving in and out of each other in the sky catching food accompanied by beautiful music. I found the whole experience very moving. What a fantastic day out which had a lovely finishing touch. As I was walking back I had to move to the side of the path to let numerous folk go by mounted on absolutely magnificent Shire Horses, they were such beautiful brown gentle giants with their enormous feet clothed in long white shaggy hair.

Time to move on again, this time to a private site at Troutbeck not far from Keswick. I had decided that I needed a bit of a break from driving and so I booked for a whole week's stay as I was told it was a nice site and it was perfect for exploring the area.

After a fond farewell with the Scottish couple I was back on the road again but it was a fairly straightforward route and apart from the rain and having to pull over on a number of occasions to let traffic pass me (there wasn't much dual carriageway) it was pretty stress free. I arrived at the site in the early afternoon and despite the low cloud I could tell the scenery all around was incredible. I had a pitch right next to a small meandering river which gurgled away as the water passed over the stones and which eventually ran into the Derwentwater and although it was so murky that I couldn't see the tops, I could tell there were mountains all around. The only downside was it was quite a long walk to the facilities and the 'well-stocked' shop was anything but because they had had a problem with their fridge/freezer. I resorted to Cheesy Cheddars for supper. One of the other pluses of this site was that I could get a really good Wi-Fi signal and so I could watch BBC Iplayer on my laptop which was wonderful especially as that first night I was stuck in Daisy as it was too wet to sit outside.

The morning was still pretty grim and so I caught up on emails, also I had some tremendous news. Jo phoned to say that she had passed her degree. I was so proud of her because I knew how much effort she had put in and how difficult it is for a working mum like her to achieve this.

The sun finally came out after lunch and so I could go out walking plus I could see the Cumbrian Mountains in their full splendour, wow! There was a great walk from the site along the lane to Stathes where I found a pub and so of course I had to partake of a lager with a bag of crisps to accompany it. You could do a serious walk from here up one of the mountains but it was very steep and I didn't like the idea of doing it on my own in case I got injured or lost. Instead I wandered back and sat by the river in the sunshine and read.

As there was a bus stop not far from the site, the next day I caught the bus to Keswick which was a very good move as Keswick is really busy in July/August although not as bad as Windermere. However, parking was still difficult. I really enjoyed looking around Keswick and I ended up going two days running as there was so much to do there. It is surrounded by mountains and the centre of Keswick is pedestrianised so you can walk around without fear of being run over, it is also where they hold the market. It has two parks as well as Lake Derwentwater. I did a boat trip around the lake which takes about an hour as it isn't as big as Lake Windermere but I thought it just as beautiful. You go past the island where they filmed Swallows and Amazons. I got chatting to a delightful lady who sat next to me on the boat who was very knowledgeable about the district and so we had a very interesting conversation. As well as passing on what she knew of the area, she was telling me about a book she was reading written by the MP at the time for Penrith about Afghanistan, it sounded really good. I hadn't the nerve to share with her what I was reading at the time as I felt I may give a bad impression, it was a very silly but enjoyable book by Sophie Kinsella.

The second day I went into Keswick, it was market day and so really busy but it was an excellent market and so I stocked up with all sorts of goodies. My plan was to walk around the lake to the landing stage and then follow the N.T. path up to Cat Bells but it wasn't quite so simple as that. All went well to start with walking through the woods and then I followed the path alongside some beaches on the lakeside. The path then followed an area where a pathway had been cut through bamboo which I assumed continued on alongside the lake. However, I suddenly found myself in a swamp area completely surrounded by tall plants and so I couldn't see where I was. I actually started to feel quite scared as my imagination ran wild and I had convinced myself that I was going to sink without trace in the swamp. In the end I felt terrible as the only thing I could do was trample down some plants until I reached a field, I didn't dare look back to see what damage I had done. I should have bought a weekly pass for the launch which takes you to the various landing stations. I could have explored from them which would have been a lot safer. I did discover where the CCC site is though, I knew it was by a lake and it was very well situated but very popular and so I couldn't book in there as it was full. I assume that this was why I couldn't find my way around the lake as it is cut off at this point from the public. I will know for next time.

I eventually found my way back to the park and looked at what was on at the theatre but they only did matinees during August and the buses didn't work for me to attend an evening performance. I had had a great couple of days exploring Keswick, the only slightly disconcerting thing was, there were armed policemen walking around which is a pretty unusual sight in this country. Plus, when trying to get Wi-Fi sorted at the site it came up with MI5 Surveillance, how strange. My imagination ran wild again and I started to think that maybe they were expecting a terrorist attack but all remained peaceful.

The weather had become really hot and sunny again and so I stayed on the site for a laundry/clean-up day. Cleaning Daisy was a doddle compared to the house. Afterwards I spent the day relaxing, reading and drawing. My sketch of the mountains wasn't too bad even though I say it myself but the sketch of the river was a disaster. How do you draw water as it passes over rocks and flows on? My effort certainly didn't portray the reality of the beautiful water with the sun shining on it, tinkling as it flowed over the rocks. The absolute delight of the day was spotting a Red Squirrel. I had read that they could be seen around here but I hadn't dared to hope that I would see one. So special! Such a beautiful creature! It stopped and looked at me for quite a few moments before running off. I had hoped on that evening that I would see the eclipse of the moon which, if visible, should have been blood red. After a perfect day of clear blue skies the inevitable happened and by the time the eclipse should have been visible, the clouds came over and then the thunder and lightning storm started. I was really disappointed not to see the eclipse but I was compensated to some extent by the spectacular lightning display, the fork and sheet lightning within the mountains, the thunder was deafening. It went on for quite some time and I just hoped that Daisy's rubber tyres would protect me in the van if it got struck.

The weather had changed again and it poured for two days. Not to be put off by a bit of rain, I caught the bus to Cockermouth with a view to visiting the N.T. house where Wordsworth grew up. I didn't feel as though I could come to this part of the country and not make a connection in some way with this great poet. It was a lovely bus ride all the way there passing lakes and beautiful countryside, a joy in itself even in the murky grey light. Cockermouth is a lovely small town and the house where Wordsworth grew up was a delight. A huge Georgian Mansion with gardens that would have gone down to the river at one time. Wordsworth's father was a land agent and the house belonged to the milord of the time. The rooms were of perfect proportions and very light, volunteers had lit the fire in the kitchen and were cooking in there providing a homely aroma which permeated the house. I looked around the gardens in the pouring rain but they were worth getting wet for. It was very much a cottage garden with lots of apple trees and perennial garden plants (a riot of colour in fine weather) and then slates had been positioned around the borders with Wordsworth's poetry written on them. I can imagine it would have been a great place to grow up, you get the impression he had been a part of a loving family. Certainly the house had a happy atmosphere and you could see why it had inspired some of his poetry. Alas, his parents died when he was young and he was shipped off to boarding school, it must have been an awful shock for him.

On the other rainy day I took Daisy out and drove to Mungrisdale Church where I managed to park her just outside the church, she caused quite a stir. The church was quite small but so warm and inviting on such a horrible day. Unusually, all the glass was clear, no stained glass at all. I suspect to make the most of the wonderful views all around, particularly from the windows behind the altar. You would never tire of looking out at the scene and if the sermon was boring you could just avert your eyes. The service here was the most memorable and spiritual that I attended on my travels. There were no clergy there, the service was led by a parishioner and a local bible study group leader gave the sermon. He was excellent, very inspiring and I certainly didn't need to look out of the window. There were times when they paused during the service to give time for members of the congregation to express their thoughts, concerns, thanks or ask for help. The leader mentioned the Holy Spirit on several occasions and I'm sure He was there with us that day, it was a very spiritual and moving experience. I felt very at home and so I stayed and had a cup of coffee.

I went to find the lake at Ullswater but it was too wet and too horrible to see much, the sky and the mountains had become one, I could imagine it would have been amazing though. My waterproof trousers were really put to the test as I walked up to the Avia Falls, a N.T. Site, fantastic, no shortage of water coming down them. It was a magical walk but I got absolutely drenched. I thought Cornish rain to be the wettest in the country but I have to say the rain in the Lakes is certainly a contender. Another great day!

I had had a brilliant week in the Lake District, I had often wondered where I would want to live if I ever left Cornwall and I think it would be the Lakes. There is so much to do and the scenery is breathtaking, I had seen it in all its glory in perfect sunshine, I had experienced the angry storms and also its atmospheric rainy days.

My next stop, Haltwhistle, Northumberland. A fairly easy drive to the CCC site which was again situated by a river. The idea of stopping here was to explore more of Hadrian's Wall.

At last the rain had stopped and the sun had come out again albeit there was quite a chilly wind. I spent a fascinating day learning about the Roman occupation in these parts and about the wall. I left Daisy at The Sill (so named because the wall is built on the famous crags of Whin Sill) and then walked along the wall to Housesteads. It was only about two or three miles but it felt so much longer because it was very up and down, the 'ups' were fine but I confess I didn't like the 'downs' as they were really steep in places with rocks to walk down on but nothing to hold onto. I'm ashamed to say that I resorted to going down on my bottom at one point. Heights aren't one of my strong points and there was quite a strong wind plus sometimes there was a really steep drop down at the side. The views from the wall are truly amazing though, a great panoramic view, such a great experience. I did think of the poor people who had to build it, it must have been back breaking work.

Housesteads Roman Fort is built on a dramatic escarpment, it is described as 'taking you back to the Roman Empire'. From the remains you can clearly see where the barracks and the hospital were. I went into the mini cinema where you can do the journey back through time (very well worth doing) I learnt so much. I had no idea that the Romans always built forts to the same design, they were very civilised with communal toilets that led to a cess pit which was cleared by running water from the hill. There was a hospital with doctors and surgeons plus underfloor heating to the baths and houses etc. as well. In fact, all that seemed to be missing was electricity. No wonder they were so successful. It's strange how the empire just fell apart like all empires seem to do. What I do find extraordinary though is, how come we didn't build on their knowledge and learn from them? I'm not a historian but it would seem to me we abandoned their legacy and returned to the 'dark ages' and it then took us many, many years to progress, in fact not until the Industrial Revolution. I caught the bus back to The Sill having spent a very interesting day.

I sat by the river that evening and chatted to a fisherman. I had spotted a funny little black bird with a white throat yesterday by the river. It was hopping on and off the rocks and then disappearing under water, I had never seen one before. He told me it was a Dipper. It was a beautiful sunset that evening and very peaceful sat by the river.

Off to the lowlands of Scotland next.

Padiham House

Lake Windermere

Skith Castle

Thurnham Hall

Lancaster Prison

Inside

Ravenglass Railway

Munster Castle

Lake Derwentwater Keswick

Troutbeck

Hadrians Wall

Part of the Roman Fort

Chapter 9

The Lowlands of Scotland
August 1st – August 17th

I would like to say that Scotland welcomed me with open arms and sunshine but it didn't, it poured with rain and there were really strong winds. I left Haltwhistle around mid-morning as I was loathe to leave such a lovely site and I had a final cup of coffee sat by the river watching a Heron and the Dippers playing in the sunshine. It was a delightful sight. It was one of my longer drives to the next site which was near to Castle Douglas and I even had to go on the M6 for a while. It wasn't a very enjoyable drive as it had become a very windy day and so it was extremely difficult driving Daisy especially when the wind was side on and then you have lorries overtaking you creating even more air disturbance. By the time I arrived my shoulders were really painful and I was beginning to wish that I had power assisted steering. Also, I was very disappointed with the site I had booked which was on a farm at the back of some farm buildings on a hard standing with other caravans, not at all as I had imagined it would be nor how it was described in the book. However, I was in a sheltered position which was just as well as Daisy was still rocking back and forth in the wind and the bucketing rain didn't relent all evening and night. I had stopped at Dalbeattie on the way and bought a beef burger and some sausages from a lovely butcher there. As it was such a horrible evening I treated myself to the beef burger which was very meaty and so hopefully not too bad for me. I was definitely in need of comfort food that evening as it hadn't been a great day but I did get to chat to my grandson, Michael in the evening which cheered me up.

Fortunately, by the time I left the next morning the wind had abated and the rain had turned to drizzle. I was travelling to Culzean

Castle and meeting up with Ann and Pete again. The route I had planned went well for once and there were no mishaps. The A75 went along the side of the coast which was beautiful even in dull conditions, I then took the A714. The first part to Girvan was lovely, a part of Galloway, most of it went alongside the River Cree, very pretty and very little traffic and so I could chug along at my own pace. The atmosphere changed as I got into Ayreshire. The road became narrower and very twisty and went up through the hills and there was more traffic. However, it was still lovely driving through the pine forest and then the drop down into Girvan was stunning especially when the huge Ailsa Craig Rock out at sea came into view, it appeared at first to have snow on top of it but it was just a patch of cloud. I stopped at Asda and picked up a few bits and pieces and then found my way to the camp site. I had no phone signal and the SATNAV didn't recognise the post code and so I was on my own. At one point I glanced to my right and there was this massive huge white hotel and then I saw a sign and the penny dropped that it was Donald Trump's golf course. It looked hideous and so out of place with the environment around it, however did he get planning permission? The next site was a CCC site and was on the Culzean Castle Holiday Park. I found the pitch which was next door to Ann and Pete overlooking the sea, perfect! Ann and Pete arrived late afternoon and we had a great evening eating, drinking and catching up on all our adventures.

The following day was grey with a smattering of rain to begin with but fortunately it cleared up in the afternoon and the cloud had completely gone by the evening and then there was a beautiful sunset over the sea. Just as well as the day revolved around finding food to cook on a BBQ.

We tested the bus system which worked really well. We took the bus to Turnbury Country Fayre Park, a route which took us past Donald Trump's golf course again. The hotel is huge but to be fair it looked as though it had been there for a long time and so he probably inherited it. The idea of heading to the park was to buy meat for the BBQ. We bought rib-eye steaks, beef burgers and sausages, garden carrots and potatoes, all at great expense but it would make for a real feast. We had a coffee there and then caught the bus back.

We did a lovely walk from the site which we reckoned was about six miles. It took us through woodland which was absolutely full of hundreds of young Pheasants, there were feeders everywhere and so it was obvious that they were being bred for a shoot later in the year, poor things. Pete did wonder if they would miss one for the BBQ but none of us would have had the heart to kill it. We eventually found our way to the beach, we looked out for seals or whales in the bay but nothing, only a few Gannets and they weren't fishing. However, the highlight of the walk was looking out across the bay towards the islands of Aran and Mull-in-Kintyre, truly beautiful. The path back led us through into the grounds of the castle which looked very impressive. It was closed by the time we got there and so we just had a wander around the grounds and we had planned to visit it the next day in any case.

It turned into a beautiful evening, perfect for our BBQ. The meats were delicious and the garden carrots and potatoes tasted as if they had just been taken from the ground. We watched families playing a game with sticks but couldn't figure out how it worked but by the time they had finished lots of children of all ages had joined in and they were having a great time. Another lovely day and fabulous evening!

We had another great day exploring Culzean Castle, there was so much to see and do. It was once the home of the Kennedy family but is now looked after by National Trust Scotland. The walk to the castle seemed to go on forever as the drive is so long. However, it was worth it. We started off exploring the old farm area which had been designed by Richard Adam (a model of good farming practice) but the area has now been turned into a shop, cafe, etc. and then on to the castle, absolutely amazing, a lot more formal than Muncaster. It has huge windows which means light floods into the rooms and provides views to die for. Adams had designed some of the ceilings and fireplaces, very typical of his style. There is a beautiful staircase and lots of fabulous paintings and furniture. There was an inlaid wardrobe and chest of drawers which were particularly incredible, so much to see that I couldn't possibly mention everything. The kitchen was really impressive, very bright and well planned but I have to say that the library didn't compare at all to the one in Muncaster Castle. Whilst on the walk yesterday we came across the room where coal was heated to extract gas which was then piped through to heat the castle, it looked like a very dangerous and dirty operation indeed. There was also a separate building away from the house which housed the munitions. We found our way to a walled garden which was huge and created the perfect conditions for growing vegetables and then the formal garden and orangery. The Swan pool was paradise for a pair of Swans where they were looking after their five cygnets. What I did find extraordinary was the 'Hen House'. This was an actual small stone house/cottage, purpose built once upon a time for a person to live in whose sole purpose was to look after the hens that they shared the house with to provide the household with eggs. It's very clean these days but you could imagine it wouldn't have been very pleasant at the time. In fact, what struck me about the whole set up was how well planned out everything was for a self-sufficient household and retinue and all very tastefully done, no expense spared.

At the end of the day we walked back through the deer park and noticed Highland Cattle as well as Llamas and there was this beautiful white Deer with paddle like antlers. What a wonderful day which we ended by getting a take-away curry. Pete very valiantly waited for over half-an-hour at the site entrance for it to be delivered (they were late) but it was worth waiting for as it was absolutely delicious. Unfortunately, it had become quite cold again and so we had to eat inside. Our usual nightcap ensured a good night's sleep.

On the whole the booking of sites had gone quite well but for some reason today there turned out to be a bit of a mix-up. Ann and Pete decided to stay an extra night and booked in because I had told them that I was booked in for that night but whilst wandering around Ayre I had a phone call from one of the wardens on the site asking me what my van was still doing there, she wasn't very happy. I explained I thought I was booked in for that night, she still wasn't very happy and so I had to eat humble pie when I got back. (She certainly gave me a hard time, not at all friendly which is very unusual for the CCC staff). However, it was okay to stay which was just as well as I'm not sure what I would have done otherwise.

We took the opportunity to catch the bus into Ayre. It took about half an hour as it went around the villages and was something of a bone shaker to say the least but it got us there and we didn't have to worry about parking. We did the mile walk along the front. There was a circus tent set up in the park area which was next to the very grand court building, which is a huge building with beautiful gardens in front of it and statues of the good and great of times past. However, the rest of Ayre didn't live up to this promising start. The couple at Ravenglass had warned me that Ayre was looking 'very tired' these days and I have to say I had to agree with them. It was such a shame because you can see that at one time it would have been really beautiful. They were in the process of building new blocks of flats along the front which you realise whilst exploring that it obliterates what would have been a view point out to sea from the old bridge going into the town. There were some very grand buildings in the old part of the town but they had been left to deteriorate. There was a beautiful Art Deco building which looked as though it was the old cinema but it had been left to go to rack and ruin and the lovely old stone church was chained up. There were one or two Georgian streets left but otherwise it was awful. There were lots of empty shops in the centre which had horrible frontages but if you gazed up you could see that the architecture above was lovely. It became obvious as the day went on that terrible planning had ruined Ayre. We caught the bus back feeling quite depressed about it.

I had now done thousands of miles and it was time to take the decision as to whether I went on up into the Highlands of Scotland or go across the Lowlands of Scotland and start my way back down the other coast. It was the 6th August and I felt it would get too cold to continue staying in Daisy after October and so I reluctantly took the decision to go across and start the journey back. Hopefully, I can explore the Highlands and Islands another time. I spent far too long in Wales but I don't regret it.

My next stop was Moffat. Having topped up Daisy's oil and checked everything was okay with her I took the A77 heading towards Ayre and then the A70 to Douglas to get onto the M74. It was quite a long way around but it was a good road which took me through some beautiful countryside and the roads were quiet although the surfaces weren't great in places. I joined the M74, no problem, and then came off at junction 15 and found the A701 to Moffat. So far, I had found driving in Scotland much more pleasurable as the roads aren't so busy and the scenery from the M74 was beautiful with mountains and hills all around. The CCC site at Moffat is very close to the town and is surrounded by hills and woodland and there were rabbits everywhere. I was very glad to arrive as for some reason one of my knees had seized up and was extremely painful. I wasn't sure what had caused it but after rest and using a painkiller spray it was fine. Lindsay rang about the church Summer Fete and rubbed it in that Cornwall had been enjoying a heat wave for weeks whereas the weather had been very mixed ever since I entered Scotland with lots of wind, rain and it was quite cold.

Getting medication can be really difficult whilst travelling and as the doctor in Keswick would only give me one week's prescription it was time again to seek the help of a doctor. Most people of my age take something to keep them going, in my case it's Thyroxine and a blood pressure tablet. I rang the local doctor's practice in Moffat and much to my amazement I was given an appointment that afternoon with no cross examination as to whether or not I was an emergency patient, unheard of where I live. I had time to explore Moffat and loved it, so interesting. I started at the museum where I found out about the local area. It was quite an important town at one time as it was a place where carriages stopped off on their way to Edinburgh hence quite a few coaching inns. Later there was a fair amount of sheep rearing and rustling over the border and then in Victorian times the trains came. It was at this time that a young girl discovered sulphurous water coming out of the rocks and so it became a Spa town. There was a special room set aside in the museum which concentrated solely on Merlin who was supposed to have grown up in the area. Who knows? Unfortunately, the church was closed like so many in Scotland and in fact I hadn't found a single church open thus far. You can tell how important and wealthy the town was at one time though when you visit the graveyard, I have never seen so many huge monuments, there was even one to a cattle man from Liverpool.

I thought Moffat a lovely town, I suppose you could say it looks a bit old fashioned because it has kept its old shop frontages but I thought it added to its charm. The town has a very wide main street with an avenue of trees and flowers down the centre and a sculpture of a ram which was all lovely although it was slightly spoilt by the cars parked all around it. The street is so wide it unusually allows for two lanes of traffic on either side of the avenue allowing traffic to flow both ways. This threw me to start with. The old shop frontages do make it really special and going into the chemist was like stepping back in time.

When I was very young, myself and other children in the area where I grew up would go around collecting empty glass pop bottles etc. to take back to the grocers where we would get a penny for each bottle returned (we were great recyclers). The pennies would then be spent on sweets which were purchased from a very special place. In a terrace of small houses in one of the streets close by lived Mrs Tallis. You would enter her house by the front door which clanged a bell as you went in and there in her front room was a dark wooden counter running up the centre covered in glass jars of all shapes and sizes. These jars contained various types of lollipops in a variety of bright colours and flavours plus flying saucers, sherbet dips, chews etc. Behind the counter were wall to wall shelves containing large glass jars of all sorts of boiled sweets such as pineapple chunks, strawberry creams, pear drops and many more varieties. It was an Aladdin's cave of the most sugary delights. The bell would alert Mrs. Tallis who would appear from a mysterious place behind a curtain.

The shop was fairly dark as there was only one small window and so Mrs Tallis looked very mystical as she waddled through to the counter surrounded by dust motes on a sunny day, a large rotund lady dressed in black with a mass of grey hair. She could have appeared quite frightening to us children but she had a beautiful smile and she always made us feel special. Being little we could only just about see above the counter and she had the patience of Job as we would spend hours trying to decide what to spend our pennies on. Looking back, I wonder how she survived financially, I suppose adults bought their sweets from her also. The reason for mentioning this is that I was reminded of Mrs Tallis as Moffat has the most amazing sweet shop, I have never seen so many jars of sweets in one place. Not at all like Mrs Tallis's dark shop but bright and welcoming with a huge array of all kinds of goodies. I took a photo to send to my grandson, Chris who has a very sweet tooth, he would have been in his element in there.

    I found the doctor's surgery fairly easily as it was just off the High Street. I had only just sat down in the waiting room when I was called in to see the doctor. I must have looked very shocked as again it is unheard of for a doctor's appointment to be on time at the surgery where I go to. Not only that, the doctor made me feel most welcome and was very caring, she appeared to have all the time in the world. After taking my blood pressure and asking me if she could help with anything else she gave me a three months prescription, this was incredible as it meant I didn't have to worry again whilst I was away. I had practically had to beg the other surgery for one week's prescription. I then went to the chemist shop with the beautiful frontage to have the prescription made up. I had forgotten that in Scotland you get your prescriptions free although because of my great age I now get them free in any case. Needless to say I was very happy with the whole experience. My only disappointment with Moffat was that the church was locked.

    Despite having two duvets on I had woken up in the night feeling really cold and so I wasn't sorry to be moving on again. I was heading for Jedburgh which was about 100 miles away. After pumping

Daisy's tyres up and filling her up with petrol, I took the A708 to Selkirk. Wow! What a beautiful road, it meandered all through the mountains with magnificent views and very little traffic. Daisy and I were very happy although I couldn't totally relax as every now again a huge truck full of timber would appear coming the other way. I stopped a few times to take photos. By this time the sun had come out and I was starting to warm up a bit. I stopped at Grey Mares Tail Nature Reserve where you can walk up to see a waterfall. I went past the Loch of the Lowes and St. Marys Loch where I stopped and had lunch. Breathtaking views wherever you looked. From Selkirk I took the A699 to St. Boswell and then the A68 to Jedburgh where I found the next CCC campsite.

I was able to walk from the site into Jedburgh along side of Jed Water. The banks of the river are very unusual in places, they are formed by horizontal layers of a reddish sandstone. I found the Information Centre down by the bus station and planned what I wanted to see and it became obvious I wouldn't be able to see everything in one day. For a small town it has an amazing history and lots of very interesting historical buildings. I started with Queen Mary's House and Gardens. The house had several floors with light rooms and lovely fireplaces and contained a lot of her personal possessions. The garden had been laid out with formal flower beds which were really pretty. You can imagine it would have been a comfortable house to live in for those times. I knew some of the history of Queen Mary but I learnt so much more on my visit here. It would seem she was very well loved by the people but then made poor marriage choices and also had enemies particularly within the Church. Of course, her final downfall was the plotting against Queen Elizabeth for which she was beheaded at Fotheringhay Castle in 1587. What a tragedy!

After lunch I visited the Abbey, Jedburgh's jewel in the crown dating back to the 12th century. You had to pay to go in but it was well worth it as again it played a very interesting part in history.

King David I was no fool and allowed the Abbotts to build it to help rule the local people. It is huge and very impressive. It was built over many hundreds of years as the Order grew and it was obviously a very wealthy Order. In its heyday it must have been magnificent. Because it was built over such a long period of time, the architecture was influenced by those periods from Romanesque to the Gothic. It doesn't have a roof any longer but a lot of the walls are still intact and some of the stone carving is very fine. There were a lot of information boards showing how it would have looked, how it was built and how the Order would have lived. Extremely well done and very interesting.

By the time I left the Abbey I decided I had had enough cultural input for one day and so I would leave the castle for the next day. After walking back I was ready for a quiet sit but lo and behold, I heard bagpipes and so I couldn't resist going to investigate what was happening. Opposite the site across the road, there was a shopping area with a very large car park. Two coaches had arrived and stopped there so that a large group of young people, all dressed in kilts etc. could practise for a performance which was taking place that evening in a nearby village square. It was quite a sight. There were a group of drummers practising their bit at one end, a brass band doing their bit at the other end of the car park and in the middle a whole group of young people practising flag waving to bagpipes. What was even more extraordinary, they were American young people from a school in New Jersey. I spent some time watching the spectacle and recorded some of it on my phone. How exciting, an interesting end to an interesting day.

Jedburgh is built on a steep hillside. The High Street which is really steep at the top takes you up to the castle/prison which dominates the area. There are some lovely buildings on the way up and at one point you look down a side street to Jedburgh Abbey, amazing. The castle itself is interesting to look around. The Castle Jail as it is now called was built on what was once known as Gallows Hill. The present castle was built as a prison in the 1820's on the site of the old castle which was demolished. It was an example of a new type of prison pioneered by John Howard where prisoners were encouraged to change their behaviour as well as punished. There were still some pretty gruesome stories though of debtors being imprisoned there and women who it was claimed had neglected their children. Other felons were sent to America or hanged, not a nice time to have lived if you were poor. The old castle had a 'bloody past' and it is a favourite location for ghost hunters.

Saturday 11th August and I took Daisy on a trip to Floors Castle in Kelso, about 15 miles away from where I was staying. I drove over the cobbled streets through Kelso to get to the castle, the entrance to which is extremely impressive, beautiful wrought iron gates with gold embellishments. There was a kiosk just inside the entrance where you paid to get in. The guy in charge loved Daisy and was surprised I was on my own. We had quite a chat. He loved motorbikes and often went to Truro but complained about the A30. The castle was fairly quiet when I arrived but it got busier later. I parked Daisy and walked around to the front of the castle, again very impressive. It is home to the Roxburgh family, they still own and live in part of it. It is just as impressive inside as outside. Although you can only visit the ground floor there is still a lot to see, each room had something special. The room which impressed me most was the drawing room which had been designed to house the fabulous tapestries. The colours were still vibrant and were on absolutely every wall some of which had even been cut to go around the fireplace and one cut in half to go around the doorway. The craftsmanship which went into the making and weaving of them was awe inspiring and I can't imagine how many hours of work must have gone into creating each one. Apparently one of the duchesses was an American heiress and had inherited them. The ballroom was also quite lovely, I could just imagine how it would feel to go to a ball there dressed in beautiful clothes, I've never been to a ball. However, I found one of the rooms really weird as all the walls were lined with cases of stuffed birds, just about every species imaginable, one contained a whole family of owls. Very Victorian. There was an interesting short film which you could watch at the end of your visit explaining what the estate does now. It seems they have a Stud farm, Salmon fishing farms, golf course etc. It was obviously very well managed. The gardens were incredible as well, they covered four acres. The walled garden was a mass of colour in the herbaceous borders and in contrast the Millennium garden was quite formal. The greenhouses were huge. I had an excellent lunch there sat outside where I could admire the rows of Agapanthus. I had a wander around the cobbled streets of Kelso itself which had an Abbey worth seeing. An excellent day out. That evening it rained cats and dogs.

Trying to get to sleep was really difficult that night as the rain was so noisy on Daisy's roof which was amplified by the drips from the trees. When it has rained previously it has been fine, in fact on occasions quite comforting but that night it seemed really menacing. I was convinced Daisy would have leaked somewhere but much to my amazement when morning finally came she was bone dry inside. It was still pouring down when I got up and I was very tempted not to go out to have a shower but gave myself a good talking to and eventually made the effort. Lots of people left that morning and I don't blame them, if I wasn't so far away from home I might have been tempted myself. However, there were a few stoic campers in tents around who were a lot worse off than myself.

It was a Sunday and I decided to go to the Jedburgh Old & Trinity Church of Scotland for the 11am service and so I put on my wet weather gear and walked into Jedburgh by the side of the river again but I took a slightly different route this time. I walked along the main road for a while and saw a garden full of gnomes which made me smile. The service was quite different to what I am used to, there was no service sheet and I didn't know some of the hymns and so I was a bit lost at times. However, the preacher had a very powerful message, 'To love your God and to love one another, if we did this we would have peace'. If only we were able to accomplish this across the world, war would be a thing of the past.

Whenever I am at a low point, something happens to cheer me up and this morning a Heron came and landed just in front of Daisy. It seemed to have appeared from nowhere, it stayed for a few moments, looked at me and then flew off again. They seem so prehistoric in flight, and then of course there were the gnomes. Also, Sunday was a day of catching up with family and friends back home.

It was still raining the following day when I left Jedburgh. Lauder wasn't far away and so I did quite a long detour towards Peebles to visit Traquair House which is situated in the Ettrick Forest, another very special place. What struck me most when I first arrived was the unusual architecture, a tall vast three storey building painted white with many windows and three turreted rooms, one on either side and one in the middle although a bit more complicated than that as part of it has a lower roofline. The original house is ancient and dates back to the 1100's, it started off as a Royal Hunting Lodge but then became the home of the Stuarts in 1491. You can watch a video in one of the cellars which tells you about its history.

There weren't many people around and so I virtually had the house to myself to explore, it was fascinating and beautiful, luxurious but homely. All was fine until I went up the stone spiral staircase to the Upper Drawing Room. As soon as I walked in I felt freezing cold and had a real spine tingling experience, the hackles on the back of my neck went up so to speak. It really shook me and so I left the room and I was fine again, it was ridiculous as it was a beautiful well-lit room. I decided to go back in as I wanted to take some photos but the same happened again and so I couldn't linger for long and I didn't get to take the photos. I have heard of other people having a similar experience but it has never happened to me before. On my way out I did ask the person on the door if anyone else had reported feeling like that but he said no and so it must have been my imagination.

The history of the house and all the people who have stayed there seemed to have encompassed all of Scottish history. My favourite character was Constance, married to, I think, James Stuart who was imprisoned in the Tower of London and sentenced to death. They were staunch catholics and supporters of the Jacobite Cause. Constance petitioned the King to free him but she heard nothing and so three days before the sentence was to be carried out she embarked on a journey which would take three days by carriage and in the snow, one of the worst winters they had known. She must have been freezing cold, tired and frightened and probably wondering if she would make it in time. The good news is she made it and gained access to her husband in prison where she swapped places with him. He escaped dressed up in her cape and left her in prison. She must have been so courageous. It didn't mention what happened to her afterwards but presumably she was released. (There was a portrait of a Lady in the room where I felt the strange sensation and so I wondered if it was her). As mentioned, they were catholics and so there is a room where the priest slept with a secret door leading to a staircase which led to the back of the house and woods so that he could escape. The chapel is beautiful and is still used today. You can also visit the 300-year old brewery outside. I had a long chat with one of the guys there and he was telling me that most of the beer they brew goes out to America. I bought some to take home as presents also one or two other bits and pieces. What a truly interesting and fascinating place. You can actually stay there.

My journey to Lauder from here was pretty dreadful as the rain got so bad I could hardly see at times but I made it and I wouldn't have missed seeing the house for all the tea in China.

The reason for staying at Lauder was to visit Edinburgh and so the next day I caught the bus which took about an hour to get there. It was pretty crowded and I sat next to a guy who owned a Guest House in Kelso. He was escorting two of his American guests to Edinburgh where they were going to catch a flight back home. He was extremely helpful and told me where to get off the bus and what to look for. It was 'Fringe' time and The Royal Mile was full of activity with stages set along the way where the Fringe people were either playing music or doing bits from their acts. It had a really jolly atmosphere, lots of young people, some of them dressed in outlandish costumes plied you with leaflets about performances. There were even two people on stilts with funny costumes on and three people were going about dressed up in blow up unicorn suits, absolutely hilarious. Unfortunately, it was raining yet again and so I made straight for St. Giles Cathedral, everyone else had had the same idea. It is very impressive but very dark, the stained glass windows are beautiful, there isn't an altar just a very plain table covered in a white cloth but there were altars in the various chapels. I was hoping to visit the Thistle Chapel which I did but it was so crowded around there that I didn't stay long. I stayed for the 12 noon service which lasted for about 10 minutes and then left, it was just too busy to get a real feel for it. I carried on walking up to the castle where I queued in the pouring rain to get in. Again very impressive with views to die for but just so busy. I did the guided tour and learnt a lot, even that Scotland had had a King Malcolm very early on. I managed to see most of the castle apart from the crown jewels as the queue was just too long. My favourite part was St. Margaret's Chapel, a charming simple building and the oldest building in Edinburgh. Walking back down The Royal Mile I watched various Fringe acts, all good fun. This was the first time I had visited Edinburgh and it probably wasn't the best time to go to visit the castle etc. as it was just too busy and also the weather wasn't very kind but I did enjoy the atmosphere the Fringe gave it. I caught the 4pm bus back to the site.

The sun finally managed to come out for a short period the following day although it became very windy. My food stocks had become very low and so I decided to have a quiet day and drive from the site to a local Co-op. Driving back, it was so scary as the wind had become really strong and very gusty causing Daisy to be all over the place, as soon as I compensated for one gust of wind another gust came. Fortunately, I wasn't in it for long. It wasn't so bad on the site as I was sheltered from the wind. I listened to the radio, they were giving out warnings about the wind causing problems on the bridge going over to Skye, thankgoodness I wasn't on it. I had some new neighbours, a couple in a caravan who had driven up from the Midlands to attend a friend's wedding which was taking place in a castle in the area. They were telling me how dry and sunny it had been there this summer, so different to Scotland. At least I hadn't had to experience the swarms of midges that I had heard so much about.

My last day in Scotland, at last a lovely and sunny day with a breeze but nothing like the wind we had yesterday. I could enjoy sitting outside again. My trip today was to Thirlestane Castle which is just the other side of Lauder. I travelled on the same stretch of road I was on yesterday but what a difference, it was really enjoyable to drive without getting buffeted all over the place. This fairytale castle dating back to the 16th century with its many turrets belongs to the Maitland-Carew family and it is described as 'one of the oldest and finest inhabited in Scotland'. It is indeed a very grand building. It has four floors but when I was there you could only look around two as the others were in a poor state of repair, still lots to see though. I understand that the family had to pay a lot in death duties at one point which meant they didn't have the finances to look after it. However, the house is now in trust and so they do get some financial help and the son still lives in part of the house with his wife and children. The ground floor was a bit dreary as it was panelled in dark wood during the Victorian times although the main library is quite light as it has lots of windows. You weren't allowed to go up the main staircase but directed up the stone spiral staircase leading to the second floor. What a difference, the rooms on this floor were magnificent. I have never seen such fine and ornate plastered ceilings especially the one in the Duke's Bedroom and the fireplaces were very ornate also, really beautiful and very light rooms compared with downstairs. I had an excellent bowl of bacon and lentil soup for lunch before I left. I stopped in Lauder and had a look around the town for a while on the way back, a nice small town.

Despite the horrible weather I had enjoyed my time in Scotland and even though I hadn't seen it at its best, I still thought it very beautiful with stunning scenery. I even enjoyed the driving despite the pot holes in the roads. I also learnt a lot more about the fascinating history of Scotland. Although I had heard a lot of horror stories about the 'clouds of midges' thankfully I didn't get to experience them. I really hope that Scotland gives up its bid for independence as it would be such a shame to go back to those days when there was such a divide.

Moving back into England next and starting my way back home.

Culzean Castle

The view out to Aran and Mull-in-Kintyre

The sweet shop in Moffat

The pipers from New Jersey

Jedburgh Abbey

Floors Castle

Traquair House

Thirlestone Castle

The view from the top of Edinburgh Castle

Chapter 10

Northumberland and Durham
August 17th – August 27th

August 17th and I moved back into England. I was sorry to be leaving Scotland but not its weather. I headed towards Coldstream, a lovely road amid beautiful countryside and very quiet. I have to say I really enjoyed driving in Scotland because it was so quiet and very picturesque. I was doing really well until I reached the A1 and then my SATNAV decided to stop working. I had stopped relying on it but it was always good to have it as a back-up. However, I had planned the route really well and so I managed to find my way to Bamburgh very easily. On my first sighting of Bamburgh Castle I just said to myself Wow!!! Very dramatic and much bigger than I had imagined, huge. I finally found somewhere to park and explored the town but I didn't go into the castle as it was so busy, the car parks were full and there were cars parked everywhere, the place was heaving with people. I picked up the coastal road which was lovely but really busy and again, going past Seahouses, there were cars parked all over the place; what a shame, I realised that I had come to this part of the world at totally the wrong time of year. I can understand why it is so popular as it is very special and beautiful. It was definitely warmer than Lauder but the wind had increased in intensity during the last part of the journey and so I was really pleased when I found the CCC site where I was staying next, a larger site and very open and so I felt as though I was in a goldfish bowl again but very handy for exploring the area. Thankfully, a fish and chip van arrived as it was a Friday evening and so I was able to have a treat for supper that evening.

There were times when I felt quite homesick and this was one of them. I had received a number of emails from family and friends and I was missing them a lot. I decided therefore that what was needed was a good walk and, since the bus service from the site wasn't great on Saturdays and Sundays, I set off from the site and walked to Embleton beach, about a 20- minute walk away. Embleton beach is lovely, a large crescent of sandy beach with Dunstan Castle sat up on the cliff to one side. It was great to be back by the sea and I spent sometime just sitting looking out on it. It was overcast but warm. After a while I walked along the beach towards the castle and carried on up to have a look around it. I discovered some really interesting rock formations there and wished I had studied geology in order to better understand what had happened. There was a stretch of smooth black horizontal rock which suddenly went up by a metre and then just as quickly down again and from what I can remember very smooth. To start with it looked as though it could have been a man-made skateboard park but on a closer look it was clearly natural. I found out later that this kind of formation is called Anticlines and Synclines. The cliffs close-by consisted of white vertical stone and yet the stones on the beach were black. Despite my very limited knowledge of geology it was obvious there had been a major happening at one time. I had a look around what is left of the castle but didn't stay long as it was so windy but the views were fabulous. By the time I had returned to the beach the tide had gone out quite a long way and so I was able to walk to Newton-on-Sea where there is a super pub called The Ship Inn. I only had a drink there but the food looked lovely, I was beginning to wish I hadn't made a packed lunch but I had to make some economies. By the time I had walked back along the beach to the site I was pretty tired and it was raining. I finished yet another book and had an early night.

There was a path over the fields into Embleton from the site but as it had rained all night I felt it would be too wet to go that way and so I walked along the road to Trinity Church to go to the 10am mass. This would have been fine apart from getting caught up in a cycle event. I am full of admiration for the Lycra clad incredibly fit cyclists but something seems to happen to them when they are in a bunch (I'm quite sure that isn't the correct collective noun for them). Some of them are completely mad and go far too fast. I suppose it is in their bid to overtake or outdo their rivals but a bit much when they are on an ordinary road not a racetrack. It can be very scary for the poor unsuspecting pedestrian minding her own business as they start to whizz past.

For the first time since leaving home I heard the sound of the church bells welcoming and calling folk to church. As a bell ringer myself (not very skilled) I can very much appreciate skilled ringers and these were obviously very good. The bells weren't just meant to call people to church in times gone by but they were also to let those people who couldn't attend church know that they were being remembered which I have always felt is a lovely sentiment. The church is beautiful especially the area around the altar. It was a lady priest who took the service and she did a brilliant job. What would the Church of England do now if they hadn't voted to allow women priests? It took years for it to happen but I would have thought they are an absolute 'God send' with so few men being called to the priesthood. Hopefully we will start to see more women bishops soon.

After the service I wandered around the village and then went back and got Daisy and drove to Alnmouth. A lovely small town set on an estuary. For a while the sun came out and at last it felt warm and so I had a walk along the beach to soak up the rays and I was able to sit in comfort outside and eat my lunch. I had a wander around the town and found the church which was pretty special and open, I loved the stained glass there. On the way back I stopped off at Craster by which time it was raining again. Apart from a small harbour there wasn't a lot to see but they had a really good Smokery there and I bought some of their smoked bacon and a smoked kipper, Richard adored smoked kippers and so he would have loved it.

My next adventure went a bit wrong and when this happened I realised that I should have done more research. My master plan was to catch the bus to Holy Island but stop off at Sea Houses and Bamburgh on the way as the causeway wasn't passable until 1.15pm. All went well to start with, the bus picked me up outside the site more or less on time and I got off at Sea Houses. A small pretty town with nice shops and a lovely harbour which was heavily populated by a type of starling, they seemed to be everywhere. I was very tempted to abandon my plan and do a boat trip to Farne Island but I really wanted to go to Holy Island and so continued with the master plan. Next stop Bamburgh. Bamburgh is a really pretty place and my first impression of the castle didn't change, it still wowed me. An amazing huge castle built of red stone set on the top of a rocky mound with lots and lots of clear glass windows, there must have been magnificent views all around. They describe it as the 'King of Castles' and I can see why. The church is delightful too; St. Aidan started a church there 1300 years ago, today's church seemed like a mini cathedral, really beautiful. Another opportunity to spend some time in prayer.

Again I was tempted to stay and look around the castle and I wish I had because I hopped back onto the bus and on talking to the driver on the way to the appropriate stop, Beal End Road, I learnt that it was actually another four miles to Holy Island from the stop although he assured me I could catch another bus to it. I had planned for arriving at a certain time in order to be able to catch the tide just right. When I got off and looked at the timetable for the other bus I would have a 45-minute wait and then there wasn't one back. Normally the four mile walk there and four miles back wouldn't have deterred me but it meant that I would miss my bus back to Embleton. Whilst pontificating on the matter a bus for Embleton came along and so I jumped on it. What a shame as it was one of the places on my list that I really wanted to go to as I understand it is very special and I was moving on again the next day. If I had done my research properly, I could have used Daisy and got to see and do everything. Also, there was a site much closer to Holy Island which I could have stayed on. I can't remember now why I didn't book the site at Beadnell Bay, quite possibly it was fully booked. However, I did enjoy the bus ride as I didn't have to worry about driving and I could see more of the coast which is so pretty and I did get to see Sea Houses and more of Bamburgh.

In the evening I was invited to go and have drinks with Jane and David who were my neighbours on the site but live on the Isle of Wight. Well, talk about chalk and cheese. Although I love Daisy she is very basic and their motorhome was palatial, they even had a proper bar. They were such a great couple though and I really enjoyed meeting them. They were telling me about where they live which is in a house which used to be part of Queen Victoria's Estate, Osborne House and apparently she had this toilet built onto their house so that she could use it for when she first alighted from the boat after sailing up the Solent. We exchanged numbers and I did actually meet up with them again when I went to visit my friend Jill on the Isle of Wight and I got to see the said toilet which I have to say isn't just any old toilet as you may expect. Their house is beautiful and in a lovely spot overlooking the Solent. It was lovely seeing them again and Jane had bought a campervan of her own so that she could travel around solo at times. She was very kind and said that I had inspired her to do it.

I was still sad about not getting to see Holy Island and Lindisfarne but I know I want to come back to this area again and I had booked to stay on a site at Bellingham and so needed to move on. I stopped to get petrol at Alnwick where there is another very interesting castle which was used for the Harry Potter films and so very popular with children. The town looked interesting as well but very busy and so I carried on as I had planned to stop off just before Rothbury to visit Cragside which was once the home of Lord and Lady Armstrong and the first to be lit by hydroelectricity. An extraordinary house, full of inventions, you could see the work he carried out experimenting with electricity using Sir Joseph Swan's newly invented filament lightbulbs. There were many other innovations that he had worked on. It is described as a home of 'wonder and gadgetry'. Again I thought about Richard who was a scientist and so he would have loved this place. The house is very Victorian, massive. Some of the rooms were huge and had sit-in fireplaces. My favourite rooms were the ones influenced by the Arts and Crafts Movement which has always interested me, they were decorated with William Morris wallpapers and beautiful stained glass windows. The reason I love stained glass is the way the light enhances the colours and each window tells a story. The grounds were pretty spectacular as well. There is the estate carriage drive, lakes, and woodland plus a rock garden built on a massive scale. What an interesting place to visit. After Rothbury I drove through Northumberland National Park. The sun came out for me and the views were stunning all the way to Bellingham with the Cheviot Hills on one side. A truly beautiful part of the country. The CCC site at Bellingham is lovely, not too big and it has good amenities.

The following day it poured and so I had a quiet day. I had a catch-up with my fellow churchwarden, Lindsay. At one time it was considered a great honour to be voted in as a churchwarden but I was asked if I would take on the position by a wonderful man called Tom, a very gentle man, who was in his nineties and really wanted to step down. It was then that I thought well, why not? I can light a few candles. Little did I know then the true extent of what the post entails, it can be anything from trying to sort out mice trouble to organising events to raise funds for a new church roof and that is apart from supporting the priest and family. Lindsay shared with me her latest experience which really upset me. We had two benches situated in the closed churchyard where people from the community and visitors could sit peacefully and enjoy the views. They were kindly donated in memory of loved ones. Poor Lindsay had been called to the church by the police where she found paramedics working on a person who had been sitting on one of the benches and had attempted suicide by cutting their wrists. The poor soul survived but had lost a lot of blood and it was left to Lindsay to clean it up. I can't imagine anything worse and I felt really guilty that she had to experience this on her own, normally we support each other in difficult situations.

Back to rain, the wet weather gear came in useful once again. I walked into Bellingham which I thought to be a very pretty village and then I walked up to Hareshaw Linn Waterfall. A really delightful walk despite the weather, by this time I was soaked, but it was worth it. There are waterfalls all the way up but the main one is outstanding with incredible rock formations in the sandstone. The Victorians built a path to it and at one time there was a bandstand where music was played, trust the Victorians to come up with something special like that. A couple who were at the top said that when they came once before, a guy was playing the mandolin. I can imagine how magical that would have sounded but the sound of the waterfall was really wonderful too and of course there was no shortage of water coming down it thanks to all of the rain. I walked back alongside of the river, super walk even though I was getting even wetter if that was possible. When I got back to the site there was a film crew who had been interviewing people about camping. Fortunately, they were just packing up to go and so I escaped. The only thing about Daisy is when you are so wet it is difficult to get everything dry if it is still raining. I had to wait until it had stopped and then dry my clothes outside otherwise she steamed up which was horrible.

Time to leave Bellingham, a site which was a certain contender for my favourite to date as the couple who were running it were really lovely and friendly and there were lots of happy children playing and enjoying themselves and the facilities were excellent plus there were lots of things to see and do. Also, I had really loved exploring Northumberland which I think is a beautiful and interesting area.

I left Bellingham fairly early as I wanted to stop off at Hexham on my way to Barnard Castle. I had planned to use the B road but it was closed and so I had to take the longer way around using the A68 but it wasn't really a hardship as it was a fairly quiet road and I went through beautiful countryside. It is clearly a Roman road as fairly straight but very up and down to say the least with lots of blind summits. Hexham is a delightful small town with an interesting history. It has a wonderful Abbey and lots of lovely old stone buildings. The shops were individual on the whole with lots of lovely things in them. I found a fabulous art shop and I stocked up on art materials plus a great butchers and delicatessen and so stocked up on delicious goodies. I also found an Argos and so I was able to buy a new SATNAV, it was larger than the one I had but otherwise worked in more or less the same way and so I didn't have to study pages of instructions, thankgoodness.

They had a really good system for car parking in Northumberland. You bought a £1 disc and you could use it in any of the council owned car parks, fantastic. In Cornwall they have become very mean about parking, not only is it very expensive but you also have to enter your car registration number so that you can't pass your ticket on to someone else if you still have time left. I thought this was brilliant and would encourage people to come into the town to shop.

I loved Hexham, a proper town with great amenities and shops. I could have explored Hadrian's Wall from here as well. The journey from Hexham to Barnard Castle was a bit tricky as it had become very windy and it was also raining, the double whammy, but I made it to the next site, as always, a good feeling of having made the journey and arrived in one piece. I had to have a pitch for late arrivals on this site which was outside of the barriers as it was a Bank Holiday weekend and the site was full but I didn't worry about it too much. At least I had an electric hook-up which was essential as not only was it windy and raining (typical Bank Holiday weather) but also it had become very cold and so I needed to use the fan heater.

At last sunshine and warmth! For the first time in ages I was able to sit outside, this makes such a difference when you live in a campervan. I had learnt that if you miss the 7.30am shower slot at the moment you may as well wait until 9am otherwise you spend ages in a queue. I was in no hurry and it was so lovely to just sit with my morning cup of tea and enjoy my surroundings plus I had become a great people watcher since I had been away. Once I was sorted I walked along the side of the Tees through woodlands which are part of a conservation area. It took around half an hour but very enjoyable and I found the path fairly easy going. The town of Barnard Castle is lovely, different to Hexham but again lots of different shops and beautiful buildings. I spent quite a long time looking around St. Mary's Church and sat and meditated for a while surrounded by beauty, quiet and peace. A good place to pray. The path takes you by the side of the castle which must have been very impressive in its day but now just a ruin. Whilst wandering around the town I spotted a poster for Bowes Museum and so I decided to go and have a look. It turned out to be fantastic, a real gem.

I was expecting the usual historic building but in fact it was a mansion built by Constance and John Bowes. It is huge, quite expensive to go in but well worth the money. By now it was lunchtime and so I started the visit by having a delicious prawn and crab salad in the cafe and then I started to explore the top floor. This floor was mostly paintings, two amazing Canalettos plus a lot of French artists' paintings. Constance was French and a great collector and so was John. John Bowes was the illegitimate son of a Milord who married John's mother just before he died. John inherited his English estates but not the title. There was so much of interest I couldn't possibly list it all but for me the main attraction was the Automaton Silver Swan which was wound up with great ceremony at 2pm to do its thing. A wonderment! This life size silver swan turned its head and reached down to both sides of its wings in turn as though cleaning them and then it reaches down to catch a fish. The other attraction which caught my attention was a history of the Catwalk, an exhibition which covered its history from the 1960's and as a teenager in the sixties it brought back some quite vivid memories of the fashion of the day. I spent all afternoon in the museum and thought as I left what a wonderful legacy Constance and John had left to the area. Probably one of the best museums I had ever visited.

Walking back I got lost in the woods, I was really scared at one point because I had no idea where I was and I couldn't get a signal on my phone to look at Google Maps. I was surrounded by trees and I couldn't find a way out. I started to panic as my imagination started to go into overload and I had visions of having to stay in the woods all night. Fortunately, I managed to locate the path which I was fairly certain I had taken and so I back-tracked on the path to where I entered the woods. I soon realised I had taken the wrong bridge by which time I was getting quite tired. Panic over I found the right bridge and found my way back to the site. Phew! I had a large G & T when I got back and cooked the steak I bought in Hexham.

Back to rain again, it rained and rained and rained. It was a Sunday and so after ringing my daughter Jo to wish her a Happy Birthday I set off in the rain to go into Durham which was about an hour away as I wanted to go to 3.30pm Evensong in Durham Cathedral. The journey was fine apart from the rain and the 101 roundabouts, they went on forever. I arrived in Durham around 11.30 and then the trouble began. I followed the signs for the car parks, the first being a multi-storey which I ignored as I was off multi-storeys after scraping Daisy's side in Wells but then I found myself entering a pay zone and I hadn't a clue as to how they worked (I'm such a country bumpkin) and so turned onto a road which took me back out of town. It was all so confusing! I decided to turn around and head back to the multi-storey but I didn't realise until I got in there that it was only for cars. There was no going back and so I had to hope Daisy would go under the barrier. I heard the roof rack scrape the barrier but I just kept going. I found a space okay and the beauty of Daisy is she does fit into a car space but then I realised it was completely electronic whereby it photographed your number plate on entering and then you paid on the way out and the barrier lifted for you by recognising your number plate (don't you just hate modern technology at times). As I was walking out there was a sign telling motorbikes not to use the car park because the automatic number plate recognition didn't work with their number plates. Oh no! Not only did I have to contend with a barrier again but what if my number plate wasn't recognised? Daisy's is higher than a car. It's at a time like this that you need someone with you to tell you to stop panicking and that it will all be alright.

I tried very hard to enjoy exploring Durham but it was raining cats and dogs still and I was worried I would be stuck in the car park forever. It is obviously a very fine small city with a cobbled street lined by beautiful buildings and shops rising quite steeply to the cathedral and castle at the top. I explored the cathedral which has Romanesque, Gothic and Norman Architecture and it was quite something, huge carved stone pillars and each area had something fascinating about it. A beautiful stained glass window sits above the altar. Apart from going to Evensong I really wanted to visit The

Shrine of St. Cuthbert, the cathedral was built to house the relics of St. Cuthbert and became an important pilgrimage destination. I spent a long time sitting in this area just pondering about everything. Unfortunately, the guided tour was full as it would have been really interesting to learn more about it. The guided tour for the castle was also full and you couldn't get in to see it otherwise and so very disappointing. I had lunch in the cathedral crypt and then had to decide what I would do for two hours in the pouring rain. I decided to leave as I was still worried about the car park. If I had been able to look around the castle I would have stayed for Evensong but I had been to the Communion Service in the morning and I had had a good look around the cathedral plus I paid homage to St. Cuthbert which pilgrims from all over the world have done for hundreds and hundreds of years.

In the end I needn't have worried about getting out of the car park. It took me quite some time to manoeuvre Daisy out of the space but I was much better now at reversing her than I used to be and the camera had recognised Daisy's number plate and so let us out, no problem. I found my way back onto the road with many roundabouts and back to the site. The rain hadn't let up all day. I felt so sorry for the families staying on the site; even if they were in a caravan, it must be very difficult being so cooped up with restless children.

I only had one more day left on this site and in fact in Durham and although the rain wasn't so persistent the showers were really heavy at times. As it was a Bank Holiday Monday and the roads would probably be really busy, I decided that I had had enough challenges over the last couple of days and I really needed a break and some relaxation and so I just spent it doing chores, reading and planning. I realised whilst here that I probably wasn't going to make it to Canterbury as it was becoming noticeable that the evenings were pulling in, it was getting dark now at about 8.45-9pm and it was very cold at night again but I kept an open mind. Also, I was becoming more and more homesick.

As mentioned previously, I will certainly come back to this area as there is so much to see and so much of interest. Northumberland National Park is a treasure for us all to enjoy and explore and the coastline is absolutely stunning.

Time to move on again.

Embleton Beach

St. Aiden's Church

Cragside

A fireplace in Cragside

Chapter 11

North Yorkshire and North Lincolnshire
28th August - 7th September

I felt better for my day of rest although I didn't sleep great as the temperature plummeted overnight, it was freezing. I was rewarded with a fantastic sunrise which compensated somehow as it had been overcast for weeks and so I hadn't seen one in ages. I thought the drive to Slingsby, my next stop, would be fairly straightforward but by now I should realise it isn't as simple as that.

Yorkshire greeted me with sunshine at last. I had planned to go to Northallerton on the A167 and then down to Thirsk but the SATNAV wanted me to take the A1, M1 and so I went along with that as the wind was really buffeting Daisy at times and so I thought that would be easier. A big mistake! All was fine until after junction 51 and then they cut the lanes down for supposed road works although it was one of those annoying occasions where the lane had been blocked off but not a thing happening. The traffic crawled along for around four miles and stopped altogether at times, it seemed to take ages. I finally arrived at Thirsk and stopped to do some shopping, glad of a break. Leaving Thirsk I took the A710 to Scarborough. As I approached the hill at Sutton Bank there were numerous signs saying 'caravans prohibited 25% incline'. There were so many that by the time I got to the hill I was totally spooked and so I turned around and took the caravan route which takes you onto the A19 to York and then off through the villages on back roads. It was a very pretty route and not a lot of traffic and so I could take my time.

Most of the houses in the villages were built out of a lovely light coloured stone, not as yellow as the Cotswolds but nevertheless very beautiful. Also by now the wind had dropped and the sun was out and so I really enjoyed the drive but this route took a lot longer and I don't know why I panicked as Daisy has easily gone up 40% hills.

Slingsby, where I was staying, was a pretty village made up of the same stone houses as the villages that I had been passing through. I had a walk in the evening and explored it. It has a lovely pub and church which was open, a nice surprise, I was able to go and spend some time in there.

One of the things I had dreaded happening whilst I was on the trip was that I became ill and that evening I felt decidedly unwell with a temperature and aching joints. I felt very viral and so I dosed myself up, had a hot water bottle and an early night. I had been so fortunate up until this point not to catch anything. The next morning I still didn't feel quite right and managed to forget to take a towel with me when I went for a shower which is a catastrophe when you have no one to call on to go and get you one. Fortunately, because I was feeling cold that night I had worn a nightshirt rather than my lacy black number and so I was able to sort of dry myself with that.

After I got over the shower incident and dosing myself up again I left to go to Castle Howard, my reason for staying at Slingsby as it was only about four miles away. What a treat! Where to start! The approach is fantastic, you drive along a very straight road which is really up and down and has blind summits for about one and a quarter miles with a view of the Howardian Hills and then you arrive at this huge Obelisk, the castle is on the left. What a place, stunning and grand. I started off with a guided tour of the outside of the building by a very knowledgeable lady who explained which bit was built when. During the Second World War whilst a school was using it, there was a chimney fire which destroyed a number of rooms at the top plus part of the Great Hall. It once belonged to the Duke of Norfolk but George Howard took it over after the war and opened it up to the public. With money raised he was able to start to bring it back to its former glory. It is still owned by the Howard family. Granada spent a lot of money on it when they filmed 'Brideshead Revisited' but some of the rooms are fake as they wanted to create a film set. There was a very interesting exhibition all about the filming etc and the actors and actresses who played the characters, I fell in love with Jeremy Irons all over again. I watched it when I got home and it really didn't disappoint. Granada created some brilliant dramas. The Great Hall is a wow! What an entrance! A beautiful painted domed high ceiling supported on decorative pillars plus a beautiful carved fireplace. It has sumptuous state rooms but for me the highlight was the chapel which was incredible, about on par with the library at Muncaster Castle. Again, the décor was influenced by William Morris and the stained glass by Burnes Jones, yet another masterpiece. The whole chapel is a work of art and is still used today and there is a resident chaplain. There were fantastic paintings wherever you looked. The grounds were equally stunning, I walked by the lake and spent ages in the Rose Garden, the perfume in here was so heady, gorgeous, I took lots of pictures. I visited the Walled Garden and got lots of ideas for a potager in my garden. It is described as a 'monumental landscape studded with statues, temples, lakes and fountains'. Beauty, beauty everywhere and I feasted on it.

I was still on a high when I got back to the site. Whilst having a cup of tea sat outside Daisy a light aircraft entertained me, it was circling around doing acrobatics. Amazing to watch, it went on for some time, what a finale to the wonderful day. The evening was pretty momentous as well because it was here that I decided I should write a book about my travels, probably seeming possible after the couple of G & T's I had had. A number of people whom I had met had suggested this but I really hadn't any experience of writing. However, I had kept a journal and I thought I could at least write about my experiences and publish it myself for family and friends. (It took a little longer than anticipated for me to get around to doing it).

It was starting to get darker earlier and so I decided it was time I got Daisy's electrics sorted so that I could use the main light again. I had been relying on her battery-operated star lights for some time but they didn't give out very much light as they were designed to be decorative only. I contacted various garages who were too busy but kept giving me the numbers for other garages to try and eventually I found someone who was able to look at the problem straight away and so I drove Daisy to a garage at Matton, about 20 minutes away. The guy there was lovely and checked everything out. When I pulled the SATNAV out of the cigar socket a few weeks ago when it went wrong (my disastrous driving day around Manchester), it was then that I had also blown the fuse. He sorted it out for me and everything was working again.

It was midday when I got back to the site. There was a NT place nearby that I could have visited but I was still thinking about the wonders of Castle Howard and so I decided to have a quiet rest of the day sat out in the sun and did some planning for the final weeks of my trip. After studying the maps and looking at the timelines it was becoming clear I wasn't going to make Canterbury which was my last place of pilgrimage but I was going to keep an open mind. It was the end of August and the nights were starting to get darker earlier plus it was becoming quite cold at night again, plus I had now been away for four months and I was starting to get really homesick. However, I had more memorable travels and experiences to come before I returned home.

On the 31st August I travelled from Slingsby to Scarborough, a fairly short drive but before I left Slingsby I had another wander around the village and church and said some prayers for my local church as interviews were taking place for a possible new priest. We had been in interregnum for quite a long time. The journey was without incident and I arrived fairly relaxed at the new site just outside Scarborough. It was one of the larger sites but very well organised.

A couple ran a small take-away and I have to say they did the best fish and chips I had had on the whole of my journey, they were delicious. Another night I had a curry which was equally good. A guy called to tell me that he had just finished a book called, 'Daisy The Cornish Campervan'; he said it was magical and he felt he had to say something as it was such a coincidence, Daisy had a Cornish sticker on her as well as the Daisy sticker. I read it when I got back and it was a lovely story although somewhat more romantic than mine. There was another VW on the site and so I went and introduced myself to Louis and Sue from London. They had bought her fairly recently, a lovely blue and white van but without cupboards or cooking facilities. They invited me to stay for coffee and we chatted for some time about the joys of the VW, it was only the third time they had used her but I hope they had many more adventures afterwards, a lovely couple.

I had decided to catch the bus from the site to Whitby but the bus stop was quite some way away, one maybe two miles and so a bit of a walk but I caught the 10.56am bus which was a tour bus and so there was a commentary about the places of interest. It went thorough Robin Hood's Bay which brought back memories of when I was a Girl Guide. We stayed there in converted railway carriages and had a great time. From what I remember I don't think we were very well behaved but I do remember that we had a lot of fun. One of my friends, Sheila, was fantastic at walking on her hands and I was so in awe of her, she could also do amazing cartwheels. It was strange as I hadn't thought of that holiday in years. Suddenly I started thinking about when I was in the Brownies before becoming a Girl Guide. I grew up in an area known as Emscote which is between Leamington Spa and Warwick. The Brownie headquarters was near Warwick Park. We walked everywhere then and without any adult supervision. The great thing about Brownie night was that we walked back past a fish and chip shop and we would go in and buy 6 old pennies worth of chips which came wrapped up in greaseproof and then old newspaper. You would make a hole in the top and then bring out the delicious hot vinegary chips (I can taste them now). The only problem was that the newsprint then would come off onto your hands so there was no way you could hide the fact that you had had chips and it probably wasn't very hygienic but at least there were no empty cartons to dispose of. Because my Brownie and Girl Guide days were so important to me, when it was time for Neil to go to Cubs I volunteered to help out. My friend Conryn was the Akalea, she was excellent, she was a PE teacher and so knew how to keep discipline but in a nice fun way. Our sons James and Neil were friends also. Another friend, Julia was Balloo. It was so rewarding when any of the Cubs got one of their badges and, of course, the camps were great fun; midnight feasts, after which the boys were like zombies in the morning, and the camp fires where we would sit around singing and eating. Conryn's daughter, Fiona and my daughter, Jo would come along with us. For some it was their first time away from home. I think they are excellent organisations and I still remember the Motto, Promise and the Law.

Motto: Be prepared

Law:

Cub Scouts always do their best,

Think of others before themselves,

And do a good turn every day.

Promise:

I promise that I will do my best to do my duty to God and to the Queen and to help other people and to keep the Cub Scout Law.

Whitby was quite a surprise, really grand in places and the old part with cobbled streets leading to the Abbey ruins and church was lovely with lots of little shops on the way. There were a number of jewellery shops selling items made out of Jet which they get from close-by. It was worth climbing the 199 steps to see the Abbey, it wasn't for the faint hearted though. The Gothic ruins stand high on the headland and are very spectacular, you can imagine how it would have looked in the past when it was a functioning Abbey drawing people to the site for devotion.

The Church of St. Mary was pretty special as well, it dates back to the 1100's but there has been a place of worship on this site since the 7th century. The Georgian interior is beautiful. The pulpit was three tiered and the pews were still boxes with doors on them, really unusual to see that now. It can seat over one thousand people as it has a gallery standing on pillars as well. The church is famous for its links to Captain Cook who worshipped here. It is also said that the

Abbey and church inspired Bram Stoker's legendary tale, 'Dracula', I could well see why. Whitby was obviously a very influential town at one time.

There is the other side of Whitby with its amusements on the pier which forms part of the harbour defences. You can walk to the end on both sides which I did because the sea was pretty calm but I can imagine it wouldn't have been a good idea in rough weather. There were lots of seats on the pier as well so that you can sit and look out across the bay. I have never seen so many fish and chip shops in one place. I really liked it, a great day out. I caught the bus back and even managed to get off at the right stop and then walked back to the site by which time I was pretty tired. It had been a lovely, warm and sunny day.

I still hadn't really appreciated how large Scarborough was or that it was in two parts joined together by a bridge and so even though I thought I had given myself plenty of time to walk into Scarborough and find the church I wanted to attend for the Sunday Service, I was still late arriving at St. Martin-on-the-Hill Church. I was delayed in any case because Sue and Louis had popped by and we spent ages chatting which was lovely and then I thought I would walk along the cliff path but I couldn't see how you could get down into Scarborough and so I asked a dog-walker and he sent me on a route which took me back to the main road not far from the entrance to the site and so again I had wasted quite some time. There were breathtaking views from the cliffs and I learnt later that there were steps leading into one end of the town which I could have used and they would have been a lot quicker. Also, I had left my phone behind and so I had no idea of the time or where to go. What a debacle! When I finally arrived at North Bay, I asked a couple where the church was only to be told it was miles away over the bridge in South Bay. At this point I should have given up but I was determined it was that church that I wanted to go to and so I set off at a fair old pace up the hill. I had to ask again as it seemed to be taking forever and I thought I would have a heart attack if it was much farther. Fortunately, I was on the right track and came to the bridge which I crossed over and then eventually found the church. By this time I was feeling very hot and bothered and the service had started and so I had to creep in and sit towards the back in the hope that no one would notice this hot, sweaty and dishevelled person coming in late. It wasn't long before the utter beauty of the building and the service calmed me and I was able to start taking note of what was happening. St. Martin-on-the-Hill, described as a Pre-Raphaelite gem, is an Anglo Catholic church and the service I attended was a sung mass. There was a choir and attendants to the priest who had a lovely tenor voice, there were incense and bells to send up the prayers to God and the whole experience was beautiful, spiritual and magical. At the end of the service there was a period of worship to Mary.

After the service I was able to take in my surroundings properly. The church was designed by the architect, George Frederick Bodley who employed the firm Morris & Co. to design the decorations. It was another masterpiece of design and beauty, the exquisite stained glass windows were designed by William Morris, Edward Burne-Jones, Dante Gabriel Rossetti, Philip Webb and Ford Madox Brown. The pulpit, fabrics and wall paintings are amazing, rich and resplendent. I spent £20 of my very limited budget on posters and cards based on the designs of the windows etc. I left feeling very uplifted and on a high for the rest of the day. I was so glad I had made the effort to go there, such a magnificent place of worship.

I was able to take my time walking back in the sunshine and to really enjoy my surroundings. The bridge which I seemed to fly across on my way to the church is fabulous and some of the buildings were beautiful. I walked along the seafront past all the hotels and B & Bs overlooking the bay and I stopped off at Peasham Park where I had a late lunch sat by the lake watching families in dragon pedaloes making their way around the island. The park had many Chinese features which were based on the willow pattern design found on crockery. An extraordinary place where families were having lots of fun. I walked back through North Bay and found the steps which led to the cliff path which I missed on the way and found my way back to the site.

Scarborough was nothing like I imagined it would be, it wasn't all amusements and candy floss, it gave me the impression of being a sophisticated town with lots of beautiful Victorian buildings and grandeur, overlooking a beautiful bay. I guess some people may find it a little outdated as it still has a very Victorian influence but I thought that made it special. I had seen it on a beautiful day but I think it would have been just as splendid in the rain.

I loved my time spent in this part of Yorkshire, the people were so friendly and I visited some beautiful and interesting places plus the scenery is amazing and the weather was gorgeous.

Unfortunately, all the walking I did the previous day left me with a very sore knee, the same one which I hurt before but once I had applied Ibuprofen, I was fine to drive. The drive to my next destination would take me on a difficult route which included driving over the Humber Bridge. I was pretty nervous when I set off as for some reason I always think something is going to go horribly wrong when I arrive at a toll booth when I have to stop and get out and go around to the booth. I suppose I worry that Daisy will conk out and I would get stuck and hold up all the traffic and become very unpopular with the other drivers. However, as usual once I got going I was fine. I left Scarborough around 10.30am, sorry to be leaving. I was on my way to Woodhall Spa, leaving Yorkshire and heading for Lincolnshire.

It took me around four hours to drive from Scarborough to Woodhall Spa as I wanted to take the scenic route which was a bit complicated. It was a lovely warm and sunny day, and more importantly for crossing the Humber Bridge, there was no wind. All my fears with regards the bridge were totally unfounded. Daisy behaved herself and I loved crossing the bridge, it was quite exciting crossing the massive expanse of water. Apart from continually checking on road numbers, it was a relatively straightforward journey and the B roads were a joy to drive on as very little traffic.

I arrived at Woodhall Spa around 1.30pm, perfect timing. Yet another CCC site which was lovely, lots of trees next to a farm with a duckpond upon which lived a huge number of ducks. I could relax again sitting outside reading and catching up with family and friends. I was still reading my book as the sun went down and I made the best of the warm weather and sat outside until gone 9pm.

I woke up that night with a very painful knee/leg and had to spray it and rub in painkillers. It eased enough to get back to sleep and I awoke to the sound of one of the duck families talking to one another very loudly, pottering about outside Daisy. I was still in pain after showering and applying more painkiller plus even with the support of an elastic bandage I couldn't put any weight on it and so I decided that the best plan was to try and rest it a bit and have a quiet-ish day.

I booked to go to the Kinema in the Woods which was fairly close to the site, a really old fashioned cinema described as being 'unique'. It opened in 1922 when Woodhall became a fashionable Spa town and had been showing films ever since. It turned out to be a great idea and experience. The cinema certainly is very unique, the interior was amazing with painted walls, art deco wall lights and very comfortable red velvet seats. The screen was hidden behind luxurious deep red velvet curtains as you might find in a theatre, it was like stepping back in time. They even still had one of the fantastic old Wurlitzer huge organs at the front which they used to use for the silent films and it still gets played at the weekends. (I was so sorry to have missed that experience, such a blast from the past). I had booked to see the second of the 'Mamma Mia' films. The film was great, quite emotional in places but still had the feel good factor of the first film and the Abba songs were brilliant, they really make you want to sing along with them. Part way through, the film was stopped and the curtains came across and a lady came out carrying her tray of ice creams. I had forgotten how cinemas used to have an interval during the film, it seemed so strange as we have become used to an interval after the adverts and trailers but not during the film. I suppose it still happens at the theatre during a play. All in all, it was a brilliant experience. They say each cloud has a silver lining and I wouldn't have gone if I hadn't hurt my knee. That day ended with a delicious home cooked salmon supper. It was the beginning of September and I realised how quickly the nights were drawing in, as mentioned before, it always catches me out as to how quickly this happens.

The following day I could walk a bit better but decided to delay going to Lincoln for another day and instead I drove to Tattershall Hall to have a look at the Holy Trinity Collegiate Church there and also the castle. This 15th century church is absolutely enormous, it really has the wow factor. The thing that strikes you most when you walk in is how full of light it is with all the huge, small-paned plain glass windows around the building, really beautiful. Part of the church was being used as a coffee place and for the sale of bric-a-brac but the area left for services was beautiful with a carved stone backdrop to the altar. The castle itself is built like a huge tower several storeys high. I used the audio guide which was really helpful in understanding the building. It started off with when and why it was built and how it would have looked in its day - it's one of the earliest surviving examples of English medieval brickwork and then you start the tour down in the basement where the servants would have lived and then make your way up the spiral stone staircase which takes you from floor to floor. There is very little by way of furniture, etc as the building fell into disrepair years ago but you can imagine how opulent and magnificent the huge rooms would have looked in Tudor times when it was turned into a palace. There were some beautiful tapestries on the walls. An American consortium bought it from Lord Fortescue in 1910, and in order to raise money, the fireplaces were ripped out and sold to an American collector. Thankfully, Lord Curzon bought it and saved the castle and bought the fireplaces back - they are absolutely wonderful. He restored the castle and then on his death it was bequeathed to the National Trust. What a noble man he was to have restored this important historical building for the nation to appreciate. As the castle is built on the flat Fen Lands of Lincolnshire, you get the most stunning views from the top of the castle. It makes climbing the numerous steps to get up there very worthwhile. What a fabulous place!

Each time you visit one of these historical places you realise what a rich and interesting history this country has. I'm sorry but I don't think that the architects of today have anywhere near the vision that they used to have or maybe we are no longer prepared to spend the amount of money required to create beautiful buildings. A lot of the steel and concrete monstrosities of the sixties/seventies are already being demolished. Anyway, I digress.

The knee was gradually feeling a lot better as long as I didn't jolt it. However, I caught my finger whilst closing up the bed that morning and so now that was throbbing as well, I was beginning to feel like a right wounded soldier. I was determined to go and visit Lincoln no matter what. I drove Daisy to the train station at Metheringham, it was about a twenty- minute drive on a B road which went through market garden territory, very flat (I was surrounded by leeks at one point). I left her in the car park (I managed to get the last space) and caught the train, it only took around another twenty minutes to get to Lincoln. Lincoln station is situated at the bottom of the hill which rises for quite some distance until you reach the cathedral and castle. The first modern part of the city doesn't rise too steeply, it is pedestrianised and has some lovely shops on either side of the street. However, when you get into the old part of the city it starts to rise dramatically and has cobbled streets with pretty little olde worlde shops. Steep Hill is really steep but then magically you get to the really old area where the cathedral is situated looking down over Lincoln.

The cathedral is immense, a spectacular stone carved building which dates back to William the Conqueror although most of it has been rebuilt over the years. It certainly has an interesting history having even been destroyed by an earthquake in 1185 (it was only completed around 1092) and then in 1237 the main tower collapsed. It was replaced by 1311 with a tower topped with a spire which was when it held the record for the world's tallest building for over two centuries. However, in 1548 the spire fell down in a storm and was never replaced. Despite its past construction problems, the present building stands proud with beautiful stained glass windows, especially beautiful are the two rose windows, one of which is the Great Rose Window, The Bishop's Eye watching over the city. There is so much to see in this incredible building. To the left of the entrance there is a small area in the wall which was opened up in the very distant past, so that the poor, and I suspect the ill, could come to the outside of the cathedral to receive help but presumably they would have had to walk up the steep hill to get there and I suspect this was to stop them from entering the cathedral itself. You go up a lovely wooden staircase to the Medieval Library and the Wren Library, both are fascinating, in fact this whole visit was fascinating, so much history. It holds another of the copies of the Magna Carta, the original of which is housed in the castle. I had visited yet another place of pilgrimage.

The castle contains 1,000 years of hidden history but it is now more of a prison with a castle wall around it. The prison was built in Victorian times to house prisoners prior to trial. It was much lighter and brighter than Jedburgh but it tells the same sad stories. A common crime here was women being charged with infanticide, so unfair. The one story that stayed with me was of a ten-year-old boy charged with setting fire to a haystack, he never got to serve all of his sentence because he died. They suffered a cholera outbreak caused by not cleaning out the septic tank. They hung people there as well, ugh! The courts are still in use but there is now a new jail. During my exploration of the castle it had started to rain quite heavily and I didn't have any waterproofs so unfortunately, I couldn't walk the ramparts which I would have liked to. I stopped to buy an umbrella on my way back to the train station but I still got very wet and so I was extremely pleased to see Daisy there waiting for me when I got off at the other station.

What an interesting week I had had!

Castle Howard and one of the fountains

The splendid interior of Whitby Church

Whitby Harbour *Kinema in the Woods Woodhall Spa*

Tattershall Hall and One of the beautiful tapestries

Chapter 12

Norfolk and Suffolk
7th - 24th September

It had been very windy for some weeks on and off and again the drive to Sandringham was really difficult because there was a very strong wind and heavy showers at times. I was beginning to get used to driving Daisy in the windy conditions and it was only about 60 miles to the next site and, so, not so bad. However, it was a pretty busy route and there was a really bad accident on the way to King's Lynn on the A17. Traffic was at a dead stop for around an hour with fire engines whizzing past. When I eventually reached the accident spot, the two cars involved looked as though they were write-offs. I just hoped the poor people inside were okay. It makes you realise how vulnerable we are when we are driving in cars, it only takes a split second of bad driving to cause loss of life or serious injury. During my time away I had experienced some really bad driving on the roads and some people were driving way beyond the speed limits, this was quite a frequent occurrence. It seems that some people must feel invincible in their cars and that the rule of law there to protect us all on the roads doesn't actually apply to them. People who in every other aspect of their lives wouldn't dream of breaking the law, seem to think it is okay whilst driving. I eventually arrived at the CCC site at Sandringham, a huge site and it was really busy because there was a County Fayre on not that far away that weekend. However, it was ideally situated to explore Sandringham.

The weather had turned cold and dreary which made living in the van a bit difficult and so I found it best to go out walking as much as possible. I used Google Maps to find my way to Sandringham House and once I had worked out where north, south, east and west were (not always obvious to me), it was very straight forward. It was only around one and a half miles away up Donkey Pond Hill (isn't that a great name?).

I explored St. Mary Magdalene Church first of all which was much smaller than I thought it would be, very much a village church but still extremely beautiful. The first known rector of the church was appointed in 1321 but it wasn't until 1861 when it was bought by King Edward VII that it became associated with royalty. As with a lot of these old church buildings there have been various restorations over time but now it is truly wonderful. As you enter by the south porch and walk down the quite simple Nave you can't help but be struck by the splendour of the richly painted ceiling of the Chancel and then the Sanctuary leading you to the magnificent altar. The altar is made from a ton of pure silver and the front panel is exquisite. The centre of the panel represents Christ appearing among his disciples with the words 'Peace be unto you' underneath, which is very appropriate as Mr Rodman Wanamaker, an American, was a great admirer of King Edward VII and of the work he carried out in the cause of peace. After his death he presented them to Queen Alexandra, a reminder to all of the importance to pray for peace. He also presented Queen Alexandra with the silver processional cross. The craftsmanship is incredible. A very noble gesture. Equally magnificent is the silver work on the pulpit. Also worth a mention is the beautiful Lily Font which was used for the baptism of Princess Charlotte. I found out there was a Communion service at the church the following day which I could go to. Before I left I prayed for peace in front of the altar.

Sandringham House is very homely and by some standards quite modest, you can only visit the ground floor but it has beautiful sitting rooms, dining room and a grand ballroom, all south facing and so very bright. The family have their very own cinema and I could imagine them all gathered there watching something exciting or funny. Sandringham was where they all used to gather over Christmas and I can see why. The house must look fantastic at Christmas time with all the decorations and Christmas trees plus it is only a short walk to the church. The museum is also very interesting, it contains a large number of royal motors and carriages not to mention an old fire engine. It was fascinating to see some of the cars that Prince Phillip used to ride around in, such a character. I walked around the lake and gardens but I didn't go into the walled garden as that was where the Country Fayre was being held and all I could hear was a lot of shooting.

A very enjoyable day.

An early start as I wanted to walk to the church again for the service. The church was even more beautiful than I remembered it. The service wasn't as uplifting as last week's, it was a simple Communion service as laid down in the book of Common Prayer but contained a part relating to the Queen as you may expect. There was no exchanging of the signs of Peace and no sermon. I bought a Guide Book as I wanted to find out more of its history. Again, the word pilgrimage was mentioned and so I had completed another part of that journey.

By the time I came out of the church I could hear that the Country Fayre had started up again. I had thought to pay to go in and have a look around but the gun shots put me off. I had spotted a number of dead pigeons on my walk to the estate plus there were feathers everywhere. I appreciate that a number of people enjoy shooting as a sport but it isn't for me even though I live in the country.

By the time I had walked back to the site the sun had come out and it was a little warmer and so I could sit outside again. I reflected on how important Queen Elizabeth has been to my life as I'm sure she has to millions of people around the world. World leaders, Governments come and go but she has been the one stabilizing influence always keeping the Christian Faith and doing her duty to the Country and the Commonwealth. I'm sure that Prince Charles and Prince William and his family will continue that tradition, it's just such a shame about Harry.

Again another very windy day for my drive from Sandringham to West Runton. I wanted to explore the coast after King's Lynn and although it wasn't a difficult route, it was very tiring trying to keep

Daisy on the straight and narrow even though I was now used to these conditions. As with my drive to Sandringham, it was stormy as well plus I got caught up in another dreadful accident. We were at a standstill for a couple of hours whilst ambulances and fire engines went flying past to sort it out. It must be so difficult for the people attending these accidents never knowing what they are going to find and then having to deal with life and death situations and at times having to witness some pretty horrendous injuries. I think they deserve a medal for doing it. Going past the accident scene, one of the cars had had its roof taken off, so chilling to think of the poor souls involved. At King's Lynn I took the A149 coastal road stopping off at Heacham and then Hunstanton which wasn't that attractive to me with all the amusements along the front but I was seeing it on a horrible day. I carried on to Brancaster Straith where I parked up and did a wonderful walk along the beach to Titchwell. You can see Seals and lots of nesting birds there in the breeding season but all I saw were ducks and geese on the ponds and an Egret. My first taste of the wild and beautiful Norfolk and it didn't disappoint.

I carried on through beautiful Burham and Holkham (I would have liked to visit the Hall there but I didn't have time to do it justice). I would have stopped at Wells-next-the-sea, I couldn't find anywhere to park but it looked beautiful. I drove through lots of lovely villages with unusual flint stone houses which I came to realise was a feature of Norfolk. Cley-next-the-Sea was delightful and there is a huge church at Salthouse. A stunning drive and enjoyable experience despite the gusty conditions.

Although it was warm, it was raining and so I had a fairly leisurely start the next day as it wasn't very inviting to get up and get going. Eventually, I went and got the bus timetables and formed a plan of action for my stay. Today I would walk into West Runton and explore the local village and find out where the bus stops are. Being of a great age I have a free bus pass which I rarely use when I'm in Cornwall but whilst away I had used it quite a lot and that morning Jo phoned to say that I had had a letter from Cornwall County Council asking about me using my bus pass and would I be returning to Cornwall? I had to ring them to explain what was happening, I guess it is unusual for someone to be using their bus pass out of the county over such a long period of time. Oops!

I finally got my act together and took off in the rain to find West Runton following directions on a map that I got from the site office. As usual I got totally lost and found myself in the middle of nowhere by a village green. I spotted my dream house, it was fabulous and in such a wonderful position, I had to take a photograph of it. The next thing a whole gaggle of geese came along, completely free ranging and then I discovered the pond with ducks on it, all absolutely charming but not where I was supposed to be. Nothing for it but to retrace my steps back to the site and ask where I had gone wrong. Apparently I had taken the directions from the main site entrance and I should have gone out of a gate through trees at the side of the site. I had never even spotted that there was a gate there, that hadn't been made very clear. Anyway, once I had found the gate I was able to follow the directions perfectly and found myself in West Runton where I found the bus stop. I explored the town and spent some time in the beautiful church there, Holy Trinity, it was so lovely and peaceful. I walked to the beach, very rugged with sea defences, I guess they get some pretty stormy seas there at times, utterly beautiful even in the rain. By the time I got back I was soaked through but so glad I had made the effort to explore.

At last the wind and rain had stopped and it was a beautiful sunny day and so I had an early start and walked into West Runton again to catch the bus to Wells-next-the-Sea. The bus was really full and so I had to stand for part of the way but it worked really well as I could look out and see all the places of interest which I noticed driving along but couldn't really look at properly whilst driving.

The whole of the coastline is pretty amazing, long stretches of sandy dunes, beaches and sea interspersed with marshes and suddenly there are ponds with ducks on them, so special. It is quite wild as well which I love. Cley-next-the-Sea is so pretty with its flint stone houses and little shops. At last we came to Wells-next-the-Sea which was even nicer than I thought it would be. I got off the bus and walked down a little lane towards the sea. To get to the beach you have to walk out around the harbour or inlet where there were a few boats bobbing about. It was once a pretty busy harbour for exporting Malt but it seemed to be mostly fishing or pleasure boats there now. You can take the higher or lower path to the beach road, I did the lower one going and the higher coming back, it was quite a way but so lovely and then when you get to the end there is a cafe and the beach. To the right there was a stretch of sand with further inlets where the tide had gone out and dunes etc but to the left there was another beach with pretty different coloured beach huts built on stilts where I presumed the safe bathing area was. All absolutely delightful. I had a coffee in the cafe and then walked back and explored the main street and a beautiful church, St. Nicholas, which I found walking on my way to find the Wells and Walsingham Light Railway. The great thing about Norfolk, there are lots of churches and all of them are open.

The steam train runs to Walsingham on one of the longest 10 1/4" narrow gauge tracks in the world, it was three quarters of an hour of pure pleasure, it was a great train ride, the hedgerows alongside the track were covered in blackberries, sloes and rose hips not to mention the fruit trees which were covered in pears and apples but all tantalisingly just out of reach.

I wanted to go to Walsingham to pay homage at the Shrine of Lady Walsingham but nothing had prepared me for what I found there. I had visited numerous churches and cathedrals on this journey, all beautiful and spiritual but there was something about this place which felt so very holy. The Shrine of Our Lady Walsingham is dedicated to Mary, Mother of Jesus and it has been a holy site for Christians of many traditions, it has been a place of pilgrimage for over one thousand years. Services are held every day and people come from all over the world to be healed. There is such a lovely story about its origin (this is taken from the Guide Book): 'It is said that in 1061 Mary appeared in a vision to a Saxon noblewoman called Richeldis and took her in spirit to the house in Nazareth where the Angel Gabriel had asked Mary to become the

Mother of Jesus. Mary asked Richeldis to build an exact replica of that house in Walsingham saying, "All who seek me there will find succour." This became known as the Holy House. The original Holy House and Priory were destroyed by Henry VIII but the Holy House was restored in 1931 by Father Alfred Hope Patten who was Anglo Catholic. The pilgrimage begins at the west end of the Shrine where there is a beautiful blue and white altarpiece of The Annunciation, showing the visitation of the Angel Gabriel to the Virgin Mary when he asked her to become the mother of Jesus, it is absolutely exquisite. By looking at this image you can focus your heart and mind on the moment that the Christian journey began. You can continue your journey stopping at all fifteen chapels, each beautifully decorated and each one dedicated to a Saint and to a Mystery of the Rosary or events in Jesus' life, you follow that journey with him. You pass the Holy Well and the relics of the Martyr St. Vincent of Saragossa who was roasted alive by the Roman Emperor Diocletian in 304AD because he refused to deny the Gospel. You end the pilgrimage at the Holy House where you can ask Mary to join you in your prayers to Jesus. It was here that I prayed for a long time and I have never felt such a sense of absolute peace. It was as though all of this journey, this trip, this adventure, had been about this moment. For the first time in my life, I could fully understand why people are called to become nuns and monks as I had suddenly felt so connected to a higher force by the power of prayer, it is difficult to explain but I felt that our lives are a journey, joy and suffering are a part of that journey which leads us into a spiritual life beyond. I really didn't want to leave and become disconnected from this special experience.

I did eventually leave but by that time I hadn't given myself time to look around the Abbey and ruins. If only I had understood beforehand that this visit would be so important to me, I would have allowed a whole day there. The whole of Walsingham seemed very holy with its ancient flint stone houses and shops selling Holy relics and you didn't go far without seeing a priest or a monk. I came away thinking it was a very special place and I had had an incredible experience, it was 'awesome' and somehow life changing.

However, it wasn't long before everyday life caught up with me again and I found myself in an amazing very modern-day farm shop which was also out of this world. I could have spent a fortune, as it was I bought steak, apples, runner beans and a bottle of gin to take back to Jo and Lee. Such a contrast to the spiritual world I had just left.

The train definitely seemed faster going back down the hill and just as I got to the bus stop, the bus came along. I got back to the site around 6pm and cooked the steak, which was melt in the mouth delicious and which I had with the beans. As I sat outside looking up at the starry sky, I contemplated on what a particularly amazing and eventful day I had had, all very much of a mystery! What seemed even more incredible was that I had undertaken a steam train ride to get to this place of pilgrimage. None of it was planned, it just happened. The experience will stay with me forever.

The nights were definitely drawing in and it was starting to feel a bit like autumn.

I felt that I couldn't come to this part of the world without having some Cromer Crab and so the following day I walked from the site into Cromer in search of some. The path took me to the top of Cromer and then I found my way into the centre where I found St. Peter and St. Paul Church which is enormous, a very imposing building which had a beautiful modern stained glass window. Having read the history it would seem that back in 1086 when Cromer was two villages called Shipden-juxta-Mare and Shipden-juxta-Felbrigg they had two churches, one dedicated to St. Peter and one to St. Paul but then by 1317 the churchyard and the village of Shipden-juxta-Mare were gradually being encroached upon by the sea and so in 1337 they demolished the church of Shipden-juxta-Felbrigg and built a new enlarged church on the site to serve both communities hence the present day church being dedicated to both saints. It was interesting to understand that the sea was encroaching on the land right back then. A feature of Norfolk is that it does have very large and numerous churches which I found to be open and there is an excellent free guide to exploring them all, well worth finding a copy. I only got to see a fraction of them.

I walked out onto the pier at Cromer where they have shows and music in the theatre at the end. There were a couple of places to eat there but neither of them had crab on the menu. I had a wander around the town and eventually found a fresh fish shop selling dressed crab. I bought a small one for £4 to have for supper which they packed with ice for me as it was a warm afternoon and I had to walk back to the site. I had the crab for supper with a glass of excellent white wine and I have to say it was well worth the walk to find it.

I travelled on in Daisy from West Runton onto Kessingland stopping off at Wroxham to do a river trip on the Norfolk Broads. The journey to Wroxham was through lovely countryside and when I got to Wroxham I crossed over the bridge which opens up for the boats and then parked up. The boat seemed huge and was fairly full but it glides along at a fairly sedate pace and so plenty of opportunity to have a good look around. The Captain gave a good commentary on the history of the broads, the boats, wildlife and habitats. We glided quietly by all these beautiful houses with gardens that swept down to the water and where geese and ducks roam at will, even the odd Heron. Where it gets wilder we saw Crested Grebes, Cormorants and lots more Herons, I was hoping to see a Kingfisher but to no avail. It would have been fun to catch the paddle steamer but I wasn't sure where that went from. It was a very interesting and relaxing hour or so.

The drive from Wroxham to Caister was fine but I didn't enjoy the journey after that as there were lots of roundabouts and the area around Yarmouth and Lowestoft was really busy. I had another narrow miss at one of the roundabouts as I had to shift to the outside lane, I was really careful and signalled for some time before manoeuvring and when it was clear I started to pull over. However, a black car came tearing out of nowhere, the driver going far too fast and sped past me. Fortunately we didn't collide as the speed he was going at, it could have been really serious for both of us. What an idiot, he could have killed us both. I decided it was best not to dwell on it. I left Norfolk and went into Suffolk to get to the next CCC site which had a shared driveway with a wildlife park, I just hoped no lions would escape whilst I was staying there. Four whole days of exploring and relaxing.

The following morning was one of those glorious early morning sunrises which makes you feel really good to be alive and it turned out to be a lovely warm and sunny day where I could sit outside the van. I celebrated by cooking bacon and tomatoes for breakfast and then set off on foot to explore Kessingland. I walked out of the drive which was lined with banners fluttering in the breeze with zebras, Giraffes and Lions on them advertising the wildlife park called Africa Live. I walked quite a way to the beach past a church where I could attend a service and stopped for a coffee. The beach seemed to go on forever and it looked as though you could walk to Lowestoft but it wasn't very easy to walk on as it was all shingle. I sat for some time watching some fishermen trying their luck and one of them had a dog which looked a bit like a sheep dog, totally black. It befriended me and kept bringing his ball for me to throw which was fun. I just sat for hours taking it all in. The sea looked brown and then charcoal but suddenly when the sun shone on it, it absolutely sparkled. I took a longer route back and found the High Street which consisted of a garage and a few shops, not quite what I expected but at least I discovered where I could catch the bus to Norwich.

The next day was extremely windy but very sunny, not a day to take Daisy out and as it was a Sunday I walked to the local church whilst listening to the church bells, they were ringing three of them. The 15th century Church of St Edmund wasn't unusual for this area in that it was huge but it was unusual in that it had a thatched roof and they were raising money to have it re-thatched. It was a Eucharist service and the lady rector did a lovely service plus there was another priest who did the intercessions. The service was excellent as was the sermon. The sad thing was no one spoke to me and so I didn't feel as though I could stay for the refreshments. However, I had had my exercise for the day by walking there and back and so the rest of the day I could relax.

I researched Norwich and found not only did it have one cathedral but two, an Anglican and a Catholic cathedral as can be found in Liverpool.

My trip to Norwich meant an early start as I wanted to catch the 8.50am bus from the High Street. Sometimes bus stops can be extremely confusing if there is more than one as I found here in Kessingland and I had to ask which of the stops was for the 146. The bus arrived on time and I was the first to get on and so I had the bus to myself for a while but it soon filled up. I was travelling back into Norfolk, it took about an hour but stopped fairly close to the centre. My first stop was to visit the castle, the keep dates back to Norman times and you can still see the layout of that part of the castle. The rest had been a prison at one time and you can pay extra to have a look around the dungeons. It has now been turned into an extremely interesting museum plus art galleries. I spent a long time in there and could have spent longer but after a couple of hours I left as I knew I had lots of other places to visit. My next visit was to the Anglican cathedral where I was just in time for the daily mass which I found very moving. The cathedral is beautiful and up there with my favourites as so bright with some exquisite stained glass windows. It is small compared to some but I found it to be very comforting. It was in this cathedral that there was a very special place where you can light a candle and place it in a spherical iron sculpture representing the world and pray for world peace. Another couple of hours slipped by and then I walked around the cobbled back streets of Norwich to find the Catholic cathedral which was also very beautiful but quite a lot darker. There were carved pictures of the Stations of The Cross carried out by an Italian artist, again I was humbled by such craftsmanship. I took the opportunity whilst there to pray to St. Anthony to give thanks as I often call on him to help me to find things I have lost. The cobbled streets of Norwich are enchanting with lots of other churches and all sorts of little shops apart from the more modern areas with shopping malls. It gave the impression of being a wealthy city with a delightful market area. I hadn't realised until I visited the museum how much of a Dutch influence there was on this and surrounding areas because of the ease of trading with them from here. An amazing day steeped in history and beauty. A perfect end to the trip was a ride back in style on the top of a double decker bus.

As a contrast to Norwich I caught the same bus the following day to Southwold. A pretty place with a lovely harbour and there is a bit where the reed beds are. You can catch a ferry from here across to Walberswick but the day I was there it wasn't working because of high winds, the sea was very choppy, brown and charcoal in colour. There were very dramatic sea defences here as well. Some people really surprise me, walking back along the beach, a young seal had got beached and a lady had taken it upon herself to sit close by looking out for it. She said she had contacted the seal sanctuary where they thought it likely that the parents had left it there because of the rough sea and they would come for it at some point. I wonder how long she had to sit there. What a very caring thing to do. There were a couple of beach cafes to be found amongst the pretty beach huts and so I stopped and had a coffee. I carried on walking towards the pier which had a couple of eating places plus shops. What was unusual was a clock on the end of the pier which was operated by water dropping down through various contraptions ending with two statues peeing, very funny and intriguing, obviously made by someone with a good sense of humour. Also, on the side of one of the buildings there was a street artwork painting of Orwell who had either visited or lived there. I explored the little streets and had a look around the church which was huge. I ended up having a delicious Calamari lunch in a lovely little pub that served the Adams beers which were brewed just up the road. I explored the town and museum and bought some mouth-watering creamy blue cheese from the deli and then caught the 4pm bus back to the site. I was so impressed with Southwold, a lovely place with beautiful buildings, lovely shops plus sea and sand. It also has an interesting history, in the museum you can find the Fossils of Mammoths and Hippos that once roamed the Suffolk marshes not to mention the Viking rudders which are over 1000 years old. I enjoyed the bus ride back and then I had the creamy cheese for supper. A great day out.

Apart from the site at Kessingland being close to the wildlife park, it also had wind turbines situated next to the site which was fine until it became very windy, the tail end of hurricane Ali, and I was in the middle of two of them, I had no idea wind turbines could be so noisy. Also, they were very annoying as they weren't in sync with one another. I decided to move on but I had very much enjoyed staying in this area.

Polstead, my next destination, was around 65 miles away. Another very windy journey but it was good as I was getting used to driving Daisy in the blustery conditions in this part of the world. However, it was a little hair raising as I approached the River Orwell to be confronted with a sign warning of possible high winds and sure enough you go up the bridge for quite a long way and the wind was extremely strong on the top before going back down the other side of the bridge, it needed all of my concentration. I did get caught up in the Colchester road system but it was okay and I ended up arriving at the next site too early. A very kind lady let me book in early and so I was able to have a relaxing afternoon. The site at Polstead was really lovely, one of the nicest I stayed on. Jo phoned to say Chris's black eye was looking a lot better!

I was woken by the Blackbirds singing and there were a lot of chirpy Sparrows close to my pitch. I was running out of clean clothes to wear again and so I had to have a laundry morning before I could do anything else. Although a lovely site it only had domestic laundry facilities and so the washing took forever. However, the chores were completed by lunchtime and so I went for a walk into Polstead.

It was a really beautiful walk with only a short distance on the road and then across farmland and through Dollops Wood. For once the map was accurate and the path was easy to follow and so I didn't get lost. The village was just how I imagined a Suffolk village to look like with a huge pond, home to many ducks and geese (the geese had young and so they wouldn't let me get too close to take a photograph) and a village green in the centre surrounded by a lovely old pub called The Cock Inn. The houses were beautiful, some Tudor with thatches and others Georgian. Absolutely charming. The church, St. Mary's was really old, parts of it dating back to the 1100s. It has a beautiful Norman Arch and the old wall paintings can still be seen, so much history. I bought a guide book which included information on Polstead Hall, a huge manse next to the church which is privately owned and therefore not open to the public. The doors to the church were really interesting and the view from the back was stunning, I could see for miles. There was a community shop, apparently one of the earliest to be set up and when I went in there were lots of jolly ladies sat having a chat, such a lovely village atmosphere. I bought some delicious cherry flapjacks which were obviously home-made. One of the features of the Suffolk villages are the beautiful painted village signs and this one was particularly beautiful. A lovely way to spend the afternoon.

It had been very windy ever since I arrived at Polstead but mostly sunny until 3pm on Friday 12th September when the heavens opened. I had taken off in Daisy to explore a bit further afield starting with Hadleigh. Hadleigh is a really interesting place with lovely walks all around. The Church of St. Mary is huge and I spent a long time in there learning about the history of the peoples and of the town, so much to look at. The East Window designed by Ward & Hughes of Soho, comprises forty-four separate pieces, the lower twelve telling the Christian story, the twelve above are the twelve apostles and above them is the angelic host and symbols, absolutely amazing. Thomas Gainsborough did a painting of the church circa 1749-1750 which clearly depicts how beautiful it is with its wood and lead spire which survives today. The picture also depicts the Deanery tower which is very grand.

Artefacts have been found in the area dating back to the Stone Age and Bronze Age, Roman and Saxon times. Throughout the medieval period it became one of the wealthier towns in the country because of its woollen cloth industry. There are certainly a lot of grand buildings. A lot of the old buildings had new frontages built onto them during the Georgian/Victorian periods. I mooched around until I found the market where there were lots of stalls. Somehow I got talked into buying a very expensive French cheese which cost £7 at the time and, of course, I then had to buy the artisan bread to eat with it. Hadleigh is a lovely town and the plus was that it had free parking. Whilst there I spoke to an Indian lady who was selling copies of The Big Issue, she was getting £1.25 for every copy she sold which didn't seem a lot but I suppose something. She was so pleased when I said I would buy one. I felt really bad for having spent £7 on cheese.

I drove to Kersey which describes itself as 'The most picturesque village in Suffolk' and it is really picturesque having lots of Tudor buildings along the main street and a stream running through the middle of it, all very delightful as was St. Mary's Church (another St. Mary's). I parked Daisy and did the guided walk around Kersey. Kersey means Cress Island. The Kersey Brook flooded a large area to the west of the village yielding commercial quantities of cress and after harvesting it was brought into the village on 'Kedges' hand pulled sledges hence 'Kedges Lane'. How interesting! This stopped in the 1990's when the brook was realigned.

After Kersey I went to Boxford, yet another pretty place with Tudor timbered buildings and another fabulous huge church which had very ornate stone carvings and a very old carved door. Three churches in one day! Prayer had become more and more a large part of my everyday life. The Indian lady had been added to my list of people to pray for which now included all those who are homeless as well as refugees. Boxford was similar to Kersey in that it had a stream running through it. Whilst I was there the heavens opened and then it poured and poured and so I decided to call an end to exploration for that day and drove back to the site. I had to try out the cheese for supper which was extremely creamy and runny and which went very well with the bread, yummy. Another extremely interesting wonderful day where I had feasted on beauty once again.

Constable country! I had grown up with an appreciation of Constable's pastoral paintings and at last I got to see where he painted 'The Haywain'. It is beautiful country all around, the drive from the site was wonderful. Dedham Vale is an Area of Outstanding Natural Beauty and driving through it I could quite appreciate why. I headed for Flatford Mill. There is even a mention in the Domesday book records of a mill at Flatford. The NT look after the area and Willy Lott's House but you can't go around it. However, I did go on the guided tour in which the guide shows you where Constable painted 'The Haywain' or at least the area he drew on for inspiration. I learnt that he didn't actually live at Flatford, his family lived in a neighbouring village, East Bergholt, and they were quite wealthy, his father owned the mill and barges at Flatford and it is recognised that Constable would have spent a lot of time there as a child. It is beautiful with the river, bridge and old mill. I spent ages wandering around and then walked alongside the River Stour to the village of Dedham, about a 40 minutes' walk. It was so beautiful even though it was a dull day. Constable went to school here. Dedham is a lovely town, St. Mary's Church (yet another St. Mary's) which dates back to 1492, has an original painting by John Constable called 'The Ascension'. As the name suggests it shows Christ ascending into heaven, it was such a privilege being able to see one of his original paintings on this day. My favourite place in the church was the South Chapel which had recently been restored as a focus for prayer and a place of quiet. I spent some time in there thinking about everything I had experienced recently. Apart from the church there was a really old building which had been turned into a great arts/crafts centre which I spent some time looking around. I stopped for a cup of tea and pottered around the shops and then walked back along by the river. Unfortunately, it had started to rain and then it started to pour down and so I was absolutely soaked by the time I got back to Daisy. Driving back to the site I became concerned about Daisy as she didn't seem quite right, she seemed really sluggish but I got back okay and despite getting very wet I had had an amazing day, I felt so uplifted by everything I had seen.

I met a lady who was staying on the site, called Linda who was also on her own staying in a caravan with her little dog. We discussed how difficult it can be travelling on your own as a woman and she again encouraged me to write a book to show that it can be done.

I woke up around 4am the next morning feeling very cold, it was still raining!

I was still a bit worried about Daisy but I couldn't bear the thought of sitting in her all day doing nothing and it certainly wasn't a day for a walk as it was pouring with rain especially as my walking gear was still wet from yesterday and so I decided to risk driving her as I wanted to visit Lavenham and go to the church there for the Sunday service. We made it but she definitely wasn't right and being a Sunday no garages were open. However, Lavenham was worth risking life and limb to get to, a beautiful unspoilt town described as the best preserved of the Suffolk cloth towns. It has so many timbered buildings, some of which looked as though they could fall into the street at any moment as their upper floors listed so much. The church was massive and beautiful and the priests and congregation were very welcoming, there was a choir of twelve and a large congregation, the priests were walking around prior to the service welcoming and chatting to everyone. This kind of welcome makes such a difference to how you feel about somewhere if you don't know anyone. I really enjoyed the sung Communion Service, the singing was so uplifting. I was invited to stay for coffee afterwards and I met a lovely couple, Virginia and Robert.

After the service I had a wander around Lavenham marvelling at all the beautifully painted buildings and then went to have a look around the Guildhall which again was a beautiful beamed building. The National Trust look after it now but during its history it has had many uses. It was originally a house dating back to around 1510. In 1510-47 members of the Corpus Christi Guild met in the Meeting Hall. The Bridewell Room was where paupers convicted of petty crimes were sent to be punished and reformed, this was between 1655-1787. A workhouse was also established in some of the rooms in 1655 to employ poor children and others to spin hemp, flax or yarn, which must have been a really horrible job, this continued until 1834. In the 19th century parts of the Guildhall and adjacent buildings were divided up into tenements for poor families. It was saved from demolition in the early 20th century by residents of Lavenham as were several other buildings.

Lavenham had prospered due to the wool trade as not only did wool get sold but also it was dyed there and turned into what was then the famous Lavenham broadcloth. It would have been a bustling town but, like a lot of wool trade towns, it would have suffered when processes changed and it fell onto hard times. This was a blessing as it wasn't modernised during Georgian times as so many towns were and of course that's to its advantage now as it retains its character. I visited another very interesting building called The Little Hall. It was built in the 14th century for a family of clothiers, enlarged in the 15th century and then 'modernised' in Tudor times. A beautiful house containing many antiques, pictures, china etc. The garden was lovely, it has a knot garden based on a Tudor design with a traditional English walled garden.

Enough history for one day, by this time I was cold and wet and so had a cup of tea to warm up. I was so glad I managed to get to Lavenham as I would have hated not to see this town as it is so unique.

Driving back late afternoon it was very obvious that Daisy needed help and I was driving to Cambridge the following day to meet up with Ann and Pete again. Oh dear! What to do!

The amazing silver altar in St. Mary Magdalene Church

Brancaster Staith beach

Norwich Cathedral, spherical iron sculpture.

The Annunciation in The Shrine of Lady Walsingham

The Norfolk Broads

The amazing clock   *One of the lovely village signs*

Chapter 13

The End of the journey

It was time to leave beautiful and wild Norfolk and the softer quintessential English countryside of Suffolk, back on the road and heading for Cambridge.

First of all, however, I needed to get Daisy sorted. I started her up and she sounded awful, not at all right. I tried phoning Ben to see if he had any clues as to what could be wrong but no reply.

I rang a local garage but they couldn't do anything until late afternoon and so I decided to take a leap of faith and set out in the hope I could make Cambridge. Looking at her petrol gauge I could see she had used a lot of petrol over the last few days. I hadn't gone that far, when I realised that there was no way that I was going to make the next site on the outskirts of Sudbury near Cambridge and so as soon as I found a safe lay-by to stop in I pulled over. I rang the RAC and spoke to a lovely guy who was very sympathetic but then told me it could be five hours before anyone could come to me. I was not impressed. I decided that I wasn't going to wait around for that length of time and continued on my way. I looked on google and found where the nearest garage was and thank God it wasn't far away. My heart sang when I found the garage as lo and behold, there was a whole load of old VW's outside including a split screen. The two guys who worked there were great and said they would have a look at Daisy straight away for me. Apparently she was running only on three cylinders which was why she was using so much petrol. Something had come off and they reckoned the engine had been tampered with because they couldn't see otherwise how it could have happened. It was very odd that Daisy had been perfectly fine on the way to Flatford and that I noticed something wrong immediately on leaving the NT car park there but on the other hand I can't imagine why anyone would do such a despicable thing. Anyway, it was all sorted out, I was so grateful to them. I was on my way again! I kept the engine lid locked after that.

It was a very pretty drive to the site on the outskirts of Sudbury. I had planned on stopping at Long Melford and Melford Hall but when I got there I found it was closed until the following Wednesday. Another place for another time. At least the sun had been shining, it was a beautiful evening, one of those glorious evenings when the blue sky of the day gradually turns to a deeper blue tinged with purple and pinks as the sun sets and then a clear black sky full of twinkling stars. That evening there was a full moon, you could clearly see its many craters but I still think of it as 'The Man in the Moon' as it definitely looks like a face, so fantastic. I even spotted the Space Station going by. The following morning was extremely cold, when I woke up I could see my breath and my nose was frozen but it then turned into a glorious day. I was able to have my grapefruit outside.

Ann and Pete joined me here for another meet up which was great, I love their company, we always have a good time exploring and they are really good at organising everything such as finding out bus times etc and so I could have a bit of a break and just tag along. We caught the bus into Cambridge, I had never been but always wanted to go there and so I was very excited.

The first college we came upon was Christ's College and we were so lucky as they were having an open day and so we were able to go in and have a look around. The gardens and buildings were beautiful and there was an area dedicated to Darwin as he had studied there. They were obviously proud of what one of their students had achieved and what a famous person he had become. We couldn't look around inside but we did go into the chapel where they were practising for a concert, fabulous music, what a treat!

We meandered around the streets of Cambridge and came to King's College. We had to pay to go in and again we weren't able to go inside the buildings but it was wonderful walking through the grounds down to the river where we watched the guys punting.

Mostly they looked as though they were professionals but there was the odd punt with amateurs in, so funny, they were all over the place, it is obviously much harder than it looks. King's College Church was wonderful, it has such a fascinating history being very much influenced by the Tudor period, the carvings on the vaulted ceiling of the North Porch include the Red Rose of Lancaster, also the White Rose of York showing links to both houses. There is a carving of the Fleur de Lys which reminds us of when Edward III was also monarch of France as were successive kings until George III's reign, our links with France were very strong in the past. Another magnificent building which took only three years to build but it then took the craftsmen and glaziers around 30 years to create and install the 26 sets of spectacular stained glass windows.

The experience of walking around both of these colleges takes you way back in time to a very different world. A very special seat of learning, how privileged people have been to go and study there over the many hundreds of years.

Apart from the college chapels there are also hundreds of different churches in Cambridge, practically one on every street corner or so it seemed. We did have a look around another church which had been influenced by Morris, the walls were covered in his wall papers but to me it wasn't as inspiring as the church in Scarborough or some of his other churches which I visited, it seemed very dark. We walked through one of the parks to a music shop where Ann wanted to pick up her new clarinet, very exciting. It had been a great day out and I thought Cambridge to be even more special than I had imagined with its beautiful ancient stone college buildings and super shopping centre and market area. However, the bus journey back that day took forever as we got caught up in a really slow moving traffic jam.

The following day we walked for what seemed like miles to find the railway station the other side of Sudbury. Eventually we found it, it was a very small station with a ticket machine. From there we caught the train to Cambridge and then changed trains to go to Ely. It all worked really well. I loved Ely, so beautiful with a river running alongside it and then a town with a few shops. We got to the cathedral by walking up from the river through parkland where a breed of cattle was grazing that I had never seen before. They had very short stocky legs which made them look like Hippos but with a cow's head, very strange. The cathedral is stunning, yet another contender with Wells for my favourite. It was difficult to see the main open area which has a beautiful painted ceiling as they were setting up tables for a function that evening but we did get to see the amazing vaulted ceiling and it has so many beautiful stone carvings, really fine. The carved pews were also very fine. We spent ages in there, so much to see and learn about. It is said that a Saxon Princess ran away from her husband and became a Saint and founder of Ely, cathedral became recognised as one of the Seven Medieval Wonders of the World. It has a connection with King Canute and it was closed for eleven years by Cromwell. History spanning so very many years.

After a scone and coffee to sustain us we visited Cromwell's house, a black and white Tudor building. Again, it was really interesting reading how Cromwell became involved in the Civil War and it begged the question - was he right or wrong? I was shocked to read how many people he and his men had killed, particularly in Ireland and although he was supposedly a Christian it would seem he showed no mercy plus he left many churches very badly damaged. All wars are dreadful but a Civil War has to be the most dreadful of all as it divides a nation, friends and families.

We spent time by the river eating and watching the boats go by and then went back to the cathedral for Evensong which was very moving, the singing taking you to another dimension. Another fascinating and great day out.

My journey was coming to an end, although the recent days had been warm and sunny the evenings were pulling-in, it was starting to get dark early plus the nights were getting colder. I said my goodbyes to Ann and Pete but I had arranged to go and stay with them in a few days' time in order for me to catch up with my other friends from Pershore. However, first I was going to Oxford to meet up with Neil and Becky.

Driving Daisy

The journey to Oxford was eventful. Before I left home I had had many driving nightmares the worst being of finding myself on the M25 motorway amongst lanes and lanes of traffic. I would wake up in a cold sweat because I couldn't find a way off the motorway and I was completely stuck and heading for the centre of London. For some reason the thought of driving in the city of London terrified me. Here I was today living that nightmare as I was by accident on the M25 in four lanes of traffic with signs to London, Heathrow etc. I prayed like mad to St. Christopher and I somehow managed to keep my nerve and Daisy was driving like a dream again. In fact I had to slow her down on a number of occasions as I was having to change lanes as I did on the M60 but it was so much easier as the signage seemed clearer and so I had more warning plus the other drivers were more giving. Eventually I saw the sign for the M40 Oxford and managed to find the right lane. Phew! I was so glad to be leaving the M25 but I was also quite proud of myself for keeping my cool. I have to say that driving on the M25 wasn't as bad as I thought it would be and in fact I much preferred it to the M60 which is supposed to be a 'smart motorway'. The rest of the journey into Oxford seemed like a doddle after that and I was very much looking forward to staying in a hotel in Oxford, luxury.

After making the decision that it was getting too cold and too dark in the evenings to carry on around the coast from Cambridge to Canterbury, I had arranged to finish off the trip by seeing Becky and Neil in Oxford and then going on to stay with Ann and Pete in Pershore to visit friends whom I hadn't seen for a while and then finishing the trip by visiting Richard's daughter, Jen and Nick, and Gracie and Rosa in Bridport.

Oxford is one of my most favourite places because it holds many happy memories for me. When I was in my early forties I joined an A Level English Literature class at college. I had to leave school and go to work two days after reaching the age of fifteen and so I never had the opportunity to study English Literature. The class dwindled to just a few of us over the year but those of us who made it to the end and took the exam became very close and when the results came through we celebrated by a day out in Oxford. Eventually it came down to four of us, Carol, Annie, Ann and myself. Carol was a larger than life character who was great at organising adventures and she was a really good cook and foodie. She organised all sorts of trips, we would find ourselves on a trip to Paris or wherever but we often returned to Oxford, picnicking in the park after loading up with delicious food from the deli or having lunch in Browns. It usually included a visit to the Ashmolean Museum (one of my favourites) or one of the colleges.

On one occasion I wanted to find where my great grandparents had lived in the Jericho area of Oxford and they said they would come along with me to investigate. Much to our amazement their house was no longer there and a synagogue had been built on the site, it was evident that the house must have been demolished. I was encouraged to ring the doorbell and much to our delight a caretaker answered and when I explained why we were there he offered to give us a tour of the synagogue. The synagogue was separated into two areas of worship, both of which had their own Covenants of the Ark with their own beautiful scrolls. Talk about serendipity, we had no idea when we set out that we would be treated to such an incredible experience. Sadly, Carol died some years ago, we loved her very much and we miss her a lot. The three of us still get together each year and talk about the super times we all had.

I digress because this trip was about seeing my son Neil and Becky. They joined me in the hotel around lunchtime but in the meantime I had been exploring. The hotel wasn't far from the river and after a false start I found a path through the Wolfson College complex to a bridge which took you to the other side of the river from where you could walk into Oxford. I walked past a boating place which was on the other side of the river where you could hire punts etc and I watched a family trying to get into one, it was so funny, I know how difficult it is to keep your balance in that situation. It reminded me of a time when I was growing up in Warwick, when my friend Sandy and myself decided to take out her father's row boat which was moored up by their small boathouse which they had on the River Leam. It must have been winter or autumn time because I remember we both had duffel coats on. The boat was tied up to the side of the bank of the river. Sandy got in ready to row and it was my job to undo the rope and then jump into the boat. I had no experience of boats whatsoever and after putting one foot into the boat it started to move away from the bank with my one foot still on the bank. Needless to say, I ended up in the water and so did Sandy as she tried to help me. I'm not sure how we got out, all I can remember is my duffel coat feeling so very heavy. We then had to get home without our parents knowing what we had done as we were supposed to be in school, we knew we would have been in terrible trouble if they ever found out. Sandy's father was a policeman and my father was extremely strict. We got away with it somehow and we laughed about it later but at the time we were pretty scared. I can imagine it would have looked pretty hilarious to anyone standing by.

Having worked out how to get into Oxford I went back to the hotel until they arrived. It was soooo wonderful to see them. We had a great day.

We took the path along by the river which I had found and had lunch at the Lamb and Lion and then a drink in the very old pub The Eagle and Child which was frequented by Lewis Caroll, CS Lewis, JR Tolkien and other 'Inklings'. It was great soaking up the atmosphere of the place and then we found our way to the cobbled streets surrounding the Bodleian Library. It was really busy with students dressed up in their gowns and hats as it was their college graduation day. Back to the hotel for a quick change and then we took a taxi into Oxford where Becky had arranged many treats.

We started off with cocktails at The Hotel Malmaison which had once been Oxford's castle but then became a Victorian prison. Very quirky, I believe the bedrooms are the old cells but I'm sure a lot more comfortable than they would have been then. After the cocktails we went onto the Restaurant Gaud where we ate fabulous food. Bear in mind I had been living mostly on omelettes and salads with the odd treat; here I sat experiencing the most wonderful culinary delights of duck with crispy kale and celeriac mash, my mouth is watering just thinking about it. The evening ended with a drink in the Bear which is supposedly the oldest pub in Oxford, an interesting place with interesting clientele. We got a taxi back and had a night cap in the hotel. A fantastic end to a wonderful day.

Another long and lingering bath before meeting Neil and Becky for breakfast. It was a glorious autumn day. The hotel provided a buffet style breakfast which included all manner of delicious foods ranging from fresh fruits, cereals, cheeses and meats, pastries and of course the ingredients of the English fried breakfast. Fortunately, we had a pretty long walk planned that morning. We walked alongside the canal path to, I think, Wentworth, and then crossed over the bridge and lo and behold, there was The Trout, a pub where Richard and I met up with Jen and Nick when he was doing his doctorate in Oxford. We crossed over another bridge and then walked back by the river towards Oxford. We stopped off at a pub called The Perch in the village of Binsey, another haunt of Lewis Caroll's which was a lovely old beamed pub with a fire and fantastic loos and where of course we had to have a quick half and then carried on walking back towards the Jericho area where we were going to have lunch.

Whilst walking alongside the canal we watched a boat going through a very traditional lock and they did it really well but when walking by the river again they had a far more modern way of operating the locks, there was a lock keeper using an electronic control panel. Fascinating. We eventually reached the Anchor where Becky had booked a table for lunch, another lovely old place which used to be a pub for the canal workers. It had a lovely atmosphere and I had a roast lamb lunch with all the trimmings which was fabulous. I couldn't manage a pudding and so Becky ordered me an iced coffee with Martini which I had never had before, I really liked it. We went back to the hotel and Neil and Becky left to return to London around 4pm. I was so sad to see them go as I had had a wonderful time and they had really spoilt me.

During my wanderings yesterday I went into the church more or less opposite the hotel and met a lovely lady (I think she was called Wendy) who showed me around the church and introduced me to everyone in there, they were flower arranging for Harvest. I couldn't get over the fact that they had their own paid clergy and they also paid someone to promote all that goes on in the church. We struggle to heat and insure our Grade I medieval church. Anyway, today they had four services arranged and I went to the 6pm service. Much to my amazement Wendy came and sat with me which I thought was a lovely gesture and the priest came to say hello. It wasn't a traditional Harvest Service but nevertheless I enjoyed it very much and the church was practically full. How wonderful! I guess it shows what marketing can do.

I left the hotel fairly early the following day, I was so very sorry to be leaving Oxford. It was October and there was a chill in the air which reminded me we were approaching the winter months. However, the drive all through the Cotswolds to Pershore was fantastic, the trees were well into their autumn colours and so I was bathed in oranges, reds and gold all the way. I had intended to stop at Blenheim Palace but I was well over budget and it was very expensive to go in plus I had visited it sometime ago and so I decided to leave it. Further on I spotted a NT sign for Chastleton House which is near Moreton-in-the-Marsh and so on the spur of the moment I followed the sign. Unfortunately, it wasn't open when I got there but as I was driving away towards the village I spotted a beautiful Cotswold stone church and so stopped to have a look. On this occasion it was my lucky day as someone had just opened it in order to put up some posters. He very kindly stayed to let me have a look around. It was quite small but had a very ancient feeling and was obviously much loved. It was decorated with pumpkins and sunflowers which seemed so right against the mellow Cotswold Stone. I would have loved to find out more but the gentleman wasn't very forthcoming and I was aware that he wanted to lock up and go.

Eventually I reached Pershore which is a market town with many fine Georgian buildings and has a large square which would have been used to hold the markets but is now used for parking. I arrived in Pershore around noon.

Although I had grown up in Warwick, I had moved to Worcester when I was nineteen. I then got married in Eckington Church and we lived on the outskirts of Eckington which is near to Pershore. We lived in a rented farm house just off the Nafford Road not far from Nafford lock whilst saving up to buy our own home. We had very little by way of furniture, I seem to remember we had a chair which we bought second-hand and a mattress but very little else. However, it was in such an idyllic spot on the side of Bredon Hill that we didn't care. The farmer and his wife lived in a lovely farmhouse across the road, I suppose you would have called them gentleman farmers. The farmer would bring me flowers from time to time and we had a Magpie that would tap on the window periodically wanting to come in. The only thing I didn't like was in the evenings you could see the rats on the steps leading to the top of the barn. We eventually managed to save enough for a deposit on a fairly decrepit old cottage in Pinvin which we renovated over time. We started a family at the same time as two of our friends and we all had boys born within a few weeks of one another. A couple of years after that we all had a second child and all girls. The friendships forged as the children were growing up are the sort that are everlasting, such a wonderful time of life. I guess this is why I wanted to return to Pershore as part of this adventure.

My first port of call was Pershore Abbey where I lit a candle for Richard and Carol and then I found my way to Ann and Pete's house which isn't far away. When I parked in their drive, which is on a slope, I was reminded that I needed to get Daisy's handbrake adjusted, Pete had to get his chocks out. That evening Ann and Pete had planned a lovely supper, Pete had made me a bread and butter pudding especially and we drank copious amounts of wine and finished the evening with one of Pete's whisky nightcaps. It had been great fun, lots of laughs.

We caught the bus to Worcester. I was amazed at how changed everywhere was after Drakes Broughton, it seemed so much more built up right to the outskirts of Worcester. They were building the new railway station and a huge Waitrose had appeared at the top of London Road. I was nineteen and supporting myself when I first came to Worcester. I worked in a beautiful old house up on Rose Hill and shared a house with two nurses in Redhill Road. All of that seemed pretty much the same, where have those fifty odd years gone? I had visited the cathedral before but I wasn't as interested then as I am now and so I saw it in a different light. It has a fascinating history as has the whole area particularly in terms of its involvement during the Civil War. King Charles II is said to have hidden and escaped from the King Charles pub. It seems the early cathedral was inhabited by monks and I was reminded of that as the deacons were walking around and stopping to pray in certain stations as though they were monks. I think Worcester has the most monuments and tombs of all the cathedrals I have visited including Etheldreda and Bruce not to mention Elgar's. The painted ceiling was spectacular as was the pulpit. So many lovely and interesting things to see. The Crypt has been opened right up and it has a number of information signs explaining the history. There is also a quiet contemplation area which was very peaceful.

After tea and cake to sustain us we walked by the river where you can see part of the old city walls and the back of the Bishops Palace. I have never seen so many swans in one place, there must have been a hundred plus numerous cygnets, apparently they are fed from the staging by the bridge. We walked by the college where Ann and Pete met and taught and where I did my IPM qualification.

After catching the return bus back we had supper in The Star pub, Richard's favourite. We walked down to the river where there was a bat flitting around, beautiful and then we had a sort of English mezze which was so good I ate far too much. This was a perfect end to a day of reminiscing and special memories.

Ann and Pete had said I could use their home as a base to see other friends and so the following day after having a wander around the shops, I drove to Eckington to visit Liz and Nils. I love Eckington Bridge which was built using a reddish sandstone and which has traffic lights because it's just a single car width, it was designed and built with carts in mind having additional passing areas for people to stand whilst the carts were going over. The flood plains of the River Avon which are on either side are flooded most winters when the bridge is closed. Liz and Nils were very surprised when I turned up in Daisy. It was wonderful to see that they hadn't changed even though it was a couple of years since I had seen them, we just picked up from where we left off as though it was yesterday. Nils had lived in Eckington his whole life and worked on the Parish Council for forty years or more. Liz is an excellent seamstress and made the costumes for a local amateur dramatic group. Their son Nick is two weeks older than Neil, and Emily a bit younger than Jo and so we spent a great couple of hours sat in their garden with a cup of tea catching up on children, grandchildren, mutual other friends and news in general.

That evening Pete cooked us supper and then Ann persuaded me to go to Scottish Dancing with her. It was very good fun but so hard, I only attempted three or four of the easier dances and managed to mess those up but I now know what a 'tea pot' is. That night after nightcaps, I fell into the wonderful soft bed and so to sleep.

A slow start and then Ann and I went for a walk through the Abbey grounds and through Pershore town to the wetland area by the river. This was a new development since I was here last, they have put in walk ways across the flood plain and planted various species of bog plants and it seemed to be doing really well. There is a bird hide from which we watched a Kestrel hunting. Walking along by the river we saw many Swans and Mallards and I found some terrific conkers to take back to the grandchildren.

I left Ann and went off to meet up with another friend Conryn. We have been friends forever, we lived across the road from one another and our children grew up together. We had many exciting outings and adventures and as mentioned previously we ran a Cub Scout pack together when the children were young. She told me that her daughter Fiona was engaged which was brilliant news. James now produces his own brand of Gin and lives on Mount Blanc in France. We spent ages talking about all sorts of things, a really good catch-up, it was so lovely to see her.

That evening Ann had arranged for us to meet up with Annie and Bill, Carol's husband at the Thai restaurant in Pershore. I love Thai food and this is my most favourite, such a treat. We ordered one of their banquets and spent the evening talking, eating and drinking. I had a wonderful time. Richard and I had our wedding reception at the restaurant when different owners had it. It was excellent then as well and the food was amazing. I called at the restaurant a week or so after the reception to thank them only to find that it had closed. There was a lot of mail by the locked door. We were told later that a few nights after the reception the owners had done a midnight flit leaving the kitchen at the end of the evening without clearing up. They had left dirty plates and pans and food everywhere and just disappeared. Rumour had it that they gambled and owed money to some gang or other. Anyway, I'm pleased to say new people took it over and it was still great.

After saying very fond farewells to everyone, it was time to move on again. I had arranged to spend a couple of nights with Richard's daughter Jen and her husband Nick, and Grace and Rosa plus their dog Bessie who live in Bridport. I was gradually making my way back down to Cornwall. As usual, I had a lovely time with them all, we did a great walk up Golden Capp, a bit cold and blustery but the view from the top is always worth the effort. I love the Jurassic Coast, a very special part of the coastline. Nick cooked some lovely food and we had lots of fun.

It was well into October by now and so the evenings were dark and it had become quite cold. I had thought of stopping off and staying at another site before returning home but I felt as though I had had a very fitting last week to the end of my adventure, catching up with the people that I loved, eating amazing food, and having a fun time and so I drove straight home.

Whilst I had been away Jo, Lee and the grandchildren had moved into the cottage and so I had a very warm welcome back. Jo and Lee looked great and Michael, Chris, Isaac and Millie had all grown at least a foot. It was soooo lovely to be back in Cornwall, back home.

I had done it! I had driven thousands of miles, seen how beautiful and wonderful this country is, every area so diverse. We have such an interesting history and stunning scenery and also I believe I had found some spiritual answers to questions I have pondered on since I was very young.

A fantastic adventure!!! I feel very privileged to have been able to do it!!!

One of the stained glass windows of Kings College Chapel

The magnificent ceiling

Beautiful Ely Cathedral

The Trout Inn Oxford

Chapter 14

Reflections

It has taken a while for me to actually write about my adventure as life was somewhat hectic for a couple of years whilst the family were living with me and then something unimaginable happened. It was discovered that, seemingly out of the blue, the awful virus Covid was amongst us creating a period of hardship and suffering for everyone. I really never thought I would experience something so awful and so life changing. However, after much persuasion I have finally written the story of my travels.

I'm still not really sure what possessed me to do this trip and especially in Daisy. You could say she was 'my folly' and it would have been much easier in a right-hand drive more modern vehicle but somehow she was an important part of it. She was extremely comfortable apart from the cold nights and she was fun. Also, she seemed to set the relaxed pace and I could park her quite easily and several people spoke to me because of her. Also, there was the camaraderie on the road, if you saw another VW van there would lots of waving to one another or the flashing of lights. I did have mechanical problems but they were sorted out with the help of some very kind mechanics and it taught me that I was capable of coping with these situations on my own although I always had a feeling I was given a helping hand. I think that Daisy helped to create much more of a sense of adventure; if it had been incident free I wouldn't have had quite so much to write about! I was asked a little while ago if I felt as though I had been 'called to do it' and I had to answer "yes" because I don't feel there is another explanation and there were many occasions when I felt guided.

So many people were really kind and helpful before I went and whilst I was away, I was often kept going by family and friends emailing and phoning. I have to say learning how to use an 'iphone' was the best thing I did, it was my lifeline not only for communication but was an excellent backup to my SATNAV with google maps and also provided me with some entertainment. Like a lot of older people I find modern day technologies somewhat daunting but I now use my phone all of the time. A while ago I would never have believed that you could hold this small piece of equipment in your hand, communicate with people all over the world, organise your banking, find your way around and it seems find out about absolutely anything you might want to know. I can't imagine how many encyclopaedias would be needed to contain all the information you can get from this one piece of kit. A wonderment of achievement and it just goes to show what mankind is capable of when minds and co-operation from all over the world come together.

If I had done more research and planning before setting off, I would probably have managed to visit the Highlands of Scotland and finish off my trip by visiting Canterbury and using the coast to get back home. I have thought about this a lot and believe that if I had lingered trying to plan I would never have gone, and also, I visited a lot of wonderful places and made discoveries which wouldn't have happened if I had followed too stringent a plan, I love the word serendipity and what it stands for. Also, I have been left with a few places to go back to and visit in the future. My map reading skills leave a lot to be desired and so I was forever getting lost but, then again, I discovered places by accident which usually worked out very well.

I completed the link to Canterbury Cathedral some time later. Whilst staying in Whitstable, I cycled the Crab and Winkle Way which leads to Canterbury. I was glad I didn't go there as the finale to my journey as I found it very disappointing. I had seen Canterbury as the final piece in the Pilgrimage (which when I set out I didn't actually know I was going to do) as Canterbury Cathedral is one of the oldest destinations of the pilgrimage routes being the seat of Christianity in this country. The gated entrance is very impressive but the reservations started to begin when I was charged an incredible amount of money to get in through the gates. Whilst in there I felt as though I was visiting a National Trust property. There were several volunteers giving tours but these were an extra £5 where in most cathedrals they were free. Somehow this didn't set the right ambience for a truly spiritual experience. I was so disappointed that I couldn't find that spirituality in there which I had discovered in other places of worship which is a shame as I was looking forward to discovering where Thomas Beckett had died plus all the other major events in British history linked to Canterbury Cathedral. I guess I shouldn't have been such a 'skinflint' and paid for a guided tour and there is no doubt it is an amazing building steeped in so much history.

As mentioned previously, I joined The Camping and Caravanning Club which was very important to the success of the adventure. I used a lot of their sites as they have them dotted around the country and I found them to be reliable with good facilities and reasonably priced. Some are in fabulous situations others not quite so good, some are small and some large. The Siteseeker book and map were invaluable as not only do they contain information with regard to their own sites but also many other private sites some of which are on farms. Two of the farms I stayed on were lovely although the shower facilities weren't good but the other wasn't at all great. The other private sites I stayed on had excellent facilities and were in lovely situations, my favourite being Lligwy Bay on Anglesey which was right on the beach. I loved it in the early morning when you could buy a bacon bap from the van and then just walk and sit on the beach to eat it. However, they tended to be a lot more expensive. I didn't have the nerve to do 'wild camping' on my own as it seems to be frowned upon to just set up camp wherever and I would have been concerned that there would have been a knock on the door and I would have upset someone plus I didn't have the facilities.

It was quite lonely at times and so I was very grateful for the occasions when I met up with Jill, and Ann and Pete, and for the time spent with Ann in Chester, and with John and Lisel in Llandudno. Life was so much easier with someone to share the planning and execution of any visitations and also a lot more fun but on the other hand when I was alone I could do and see exactly what I wished. I ate when and what I felt like, mostly very simple meals (as I said, an awful lot of salad and omelettes) but I did have treats from time to time, something special to cook and eat in Daisy or a meal out usually accompanied by a very good glass of wine. I walked for miles and so I felt really fit at the end of the journey.

The total budget for the trip was the £25,000 that Neil had loaned me but a large proportion of that went on purchasing Daisy and sorting and kitting her out. I was left with a budget of around £9,000 for the six-month trip which had to cover petrol, food, site fees, hotel stops, entertainment and everything else. I may have just about made it if I hadn't had the expense of getting Daisy repaired. I didn't spend as much on petrol as I thought I would as although Daisy isn't particularly economical, she wasn't as thirsty as I thought she would be. However, her new starter motor, which caused most of the problems, was expensive as I had to pay for two new motors and two lots of labour costs and in the second instance it involved a night in a hotel plus towage fees. I had also paid the RAC the higher rate of cover which turned out to be a total waste of money as they were very unhelpful when it came to the overnight stay, very disappointing. Although I have to say the guys who did come out to me were lovely. Added to this was the cost of getting the caravan repaired which I had backed into. I confess I hadn't budgeted for any such events.

The site fees averaged out at £15 per night. It depended on the site and whether it was in the low, medium or high season and what sort of pitch you had. I often had a grass pitch with an electric hook-up which works out cheaper than the gravelled pitches but if the site wasn't level, I did go for the more expensive pitches as I really didn't get on using chocks. Also, because I wasn't booking very far in advance I sometimes had to have what was left. The CCC sites were generally cheaper than the private sites and as a senior I got a discount.

As mentioned previously, I ate fairly frugally but did splash out on occasions as a treat. I only had two other hotel stops in the end, the one in Lancaster for my birthday and then Oxford.

I'm a member of the NT and so many of the visits I made to the historic houses were free but those that weren't NT were fairly expensive to go in. However, they were still very good value for money and so interesting and I learnt so much of the history of the island from these places, as I did from the cathedrals and churches I visited, plus I got to see many beautiful works of art. There aren't many perks to being a senior but a free bus pass for use in England is one of them and most of the CCC sites had a bus service not far away and so I used the buses to get around where possible which also gave me a break from driving which I still hate doing.

Having lived on this island all my life, I have taken it very much for granted but travelling from place to place, county to county, I realised how diverse and stunning it really is. From travelling along the Atlantic Highway and discovering more of the dramatic Cornish coastline and then into Devon and Somerset where the air seems softer with the lushness of valleys populated with magnificent trees, verdant green fields scattered with cows and sheep grazing on them, not to mention their beautiful coastline and then into Wales where I lingered far too long because of its beauty and spirituality and its powerful mountains and so many castles. The forays inland led me to discover some delightful villages and towns with interesting architecture and history. The Lake District charmed me with its lakes which have the most amazing backdrop of the mountains, sometimes menacing, sometimes sparkling and then the lowlands of Scotland where I enjoyed driving most at a leisurely pace through mountains and stunning scenery discovering its fascinating history. Yorkshire with its rolling Dales and a coastline which was different but equally beautiful and then into wild Norfolk with its unusual lovely flint stoned buildings and so many churches, gentle Suffolk with its pastoral countryside and delightful village signs. Back down into the heart of the country, Cambridge and Oxford, the seats of learning for so long, with the fabulous carved stone architecture of the colleges.

Having learnt about all the squabbling and fighting that went on before we became a United Kingdom, it made me realise the importance of remaining united.

I visited many interesting buildings, thank goodness for the National Trust which has preserved some of our great houses and other places of national interest not to mention the work it does in preserving a lot of the coastline. I visited many cathedrals and churches, places built to the glory of God quite often taking many years to build by architects, craftsmen and artists passionate about their work. The prayer-soaked walls of many generations celebrating baptisms, weddings and funerals, mourning loved ones, witnessing the rhythm of life, each with its own story and history to tell. What a treasure these places are and available for us all to enjoy.

THE PILGRIMAGE.

Is the majestic universe a chaos of madness and nothingness or an ordered scheme of progress? Is the world an accident or a creation? Is life a dream or a destiny?

I came across these questions when I was quite young, it was in one of the children's encyclopaedias. I guess these questions are what all of us humans ponder upon. Certainly, the questions stayed with me and it was the start of a journey.

What is God?

My parents weren't particularly religious but my mother would take me to church on occasions and the primary school I attended was a C of E school situated next to the local church and which was where I learnt about the Christian Religion as a child. I really didn't like the Old Testament then as God always seemed angry, I didn't realise at the time that it was because of His frustration and disappointment with how His children were behaving. However, I also attended Sunday School classes where I learnt about Jesus Christ and about the parables which I loved. I was baptized and confirmed a Christian. As I got older I started to question religion, it was the sixties, we had recovered from World War II and young people had started to challenge the old order. Like many, I became confused as to whether religion was a force for good or bad, why were there wars, why was there suffering? Did religions cause wars? Was there a God? If so why had God allowed nuclear bombs to be discovered? I looked into many of the religions from around the world and most of their teachings seemed to me to be a force for good, offering love, hope and comfort to people. It also seemed obvious that many of us follow the religion of our country of birth or that of our parents. However, unfortunately, there are those people who get into positions of power and bend religions to their will, distorting the teachings, indoctrinating people and using them to create divisions within societies, countries and the world.

Sometime ago I read A.N. Wilson's book 'God's Funeral', the title of which came from Thomas Hardy's poem which I had read previously. The book delves into a time in the 1800's when Darwinism and scientific discoveries led to most great writers, artists and intellectuals of the time turning away from God but, from what I can gather, it left some feeling bereft. Certainly, Thomas Hardy felt he had lost something precious and when he wrote the poem, it wasn't really an attack on religion but only that he felt there needed to be a 20th century version of it without the dogma of that day.

From the time of Galileo when he first put his lens to the sky and then to our modern-day Hubble telescope, we keep learning so much about the universe. I recently watched a programme about the James Webb Telescope which was successfully launched in 2022. The programme covered its conception and the thirty years it took to build, what a feat of human perseverance and ingenuity. If the mission is successful the telescope will go out to the beginning of time and we will learn even more of the wonders of the universe. How spectacular and absolutely mind boggling! I am not an intellectual by any means, my beliefs are based on a lifetime of searching and so for me those wonders don't preclude God as Creator.

When I was in my early forties I was going through a particularly difficult time, my world had been turned upside down and I turned to God for help, that help was forthcoming in quite a spectacular way and since that time I have never felt truly alone. I was still on the journey of questioning and discovering but my faith in God and Christ deepened. In the First Century, Christianity was simply The Way which meant faith in Christ and eternal life, faith in love, faith in human kindness, faith in mercy, faith in absolute unselfishness. When the Church of Rome became powerful, it gradually undertook to fix what all Christians should believe.

I had no intention of undertaking a Pilgrimage when I started out on this journey, it just kind of happened. It started to dawn on me during my time in Wales that that was what I was doing. I know there is a view that Christ never needed church buildings to tell His story from but I was always very disappointed if I found a church locked because for me they are centres of calm in which to reflect and pray and learn about the history of the area. Our cathedrals are masterpieces of architecture and beauty, and places where people from all over the world come to pay homage and look for spiritual nourishment and again centres where history is gathered. They give an opportunity to feel that extra bit connected to a higher spiritual entity.

From the time I spent in Wales and then visiting all of the other places of pilgrimage on my journey, I at last found myself at The Shrine of Our Lady of Walsingham which seemed to be the catalyst for what I had been searching. It was such a moment of complete understanding, connection and peacefulness. I found it very hard to leave there and to leave that connection behind and to return to 'life as usual', I knew I would never forget that moment. There are still times when life seems very hard but also times when it is pure joy and I no longer fear death.

History is history and we can't undo it but surely, we should be learning from it. During the trip I was appalled to see the news showing the human suffering being caused by the then war in Syria, a Civil war causing so many people to die or to have to leave their homes, travelling miles in awful conditions to find sanctuary. It became the focus of my prayers and now the same is happening in Ukraine. Throughout history there seem to be people such as, in more recent times, Hitler, Polpot, Mao, Stalin and now Putin who come to power and create so much carnage and suffering and they gather around them sycophants who do their bidding. They lie and don't care how many people are killed and if the people object they're incarcerated or killed. They seem to think in some bizarre way of their rightness and that they are saviours of their country. With Hitler, it was his obsession with 'The Fatherland' and now Putin with 'The Motherland'. How do we ever stop this from happening? If we followed those early teachings of Christianity, to love God and one another, faith in love, faith in human kindness, faith in mercy and faith in absolute unselfishness then the world would be such a better place, we would be helping and working together to build a better future for us all and for generations to come and to care for this amazing, fabulous planet rather than fighting one another over it.

I am aware that I have used the words, beautiful, incredible, stunning, amazing, wonderful, fantastic an awful lot and in fact I ran out of words to describe the beauty I was seeing on my journey. I'm not well travelled but just experiencing the wonders and beauty here in this country and from what I've seen of the wonders and beauty in other countries, we do live in a wondrous world which is a part of a wondrous universe.

We are all part of God's creation and He loves us, we are His children, His loving Spirit is within us which we can reach if we open our hearts and minds and then the Holy Spirit is all around us. I'm certain that life is a 'destiny' and not a 'dream'.

The message sent through Christ is simple, Love God and each other. Atheism (the belief or doctrine that there is no deity) seems to becoming the more fashionable religion today in this country but I could never be an atheist as that is such a lonely path to follow. An easier path to follow for sure as The Way of Christ is difficult and as we are human we find it easy to stray from the path and hurt one another but if we just tried harder to love and help one another then peace would surely come. 'Peace, blessed word, easily spoken but the one thing since the beginning of history the world has found it most difficult to keep and enjoy.'

I would like to share with you the prayer 'Footprints' which I think probably describes best what I have been trying to say:

One night a man had a dream

He walked along a beach, the Lord at his side,

Across the sky flashed scenes from his life....

...He saw two sets of footprints in the sand,

his own and those of the Lord.

But looking back he noticed at times along

the path, there was only one set of footprints.

This was often at difficult times of his life...

...He asked, "My Lord, you said that if I

follow you, you would walk with me all the way,

But in times of trouble there is only one set

of footprints. Why have you left me when

I needed you the most?"...

... The Lord answered, "My precious child,

I love you and I would never leave you.

During your times of trial,

when you see only one set of footprints,

that's when I was carrying you."

I would also like to share a poem written by the Reverend Studdert Kennedy, a padre serving in the First World War known by the men as Woodbine Willie. He was surrounded by unimaginable suffering and horrors but he was still able to see beauty.

The Unutterable Beauty

God, give me speech, in mercy touch my lips,
I cannot bear Thy Beauty and be still.
Watching the red-gold majesty that tips
The crest of yonder hill,
And out to sea smites on the sails of ships.

That flame like drifting stars across the deep,
Calling their silver comrades from the sky,
As long and ever longer shadows creep,
To sing their lullaby,
And hush the tired eyes of earth to sleep.

Thy radiancy of glory strikes me dumb,
Yet cries within my soul for power to raise
Such miracles of music as would sum
Thy splendour in a phrase
Storing it safe for all the years to come.

O God, Who givest songs too sweet to sing,
Have mercy on Thy servant's feeble tongue,
In sacrificial silence unsung,
Accepted at Thy mercy-seat, may bring

New light into the darkness of sad eyes,

New tenderness to stay the stream of tears,

New rainbows from the sunshine of surprise,

To guide men down the years,

Until they cross the last long bridge of sighs.

I still haven't discovered all of the answers to the questions by any means but I have now discovered enough to have absolute faith in 'God' and the teachings of Christianity. I love to go to church to regain that spiritual connection, I love the beauty of the surroundings and to learn and to share.

Little did I realise when I started out on this 'adventure' that I would be writing this last chapter.

It was an amazing 'adventure/pilgrimage', a life changing experience!

Acknowledgements

I would like to thank all of my family and friends who supported me in this adventure and Paul for his 'technical support', I couldn't have done it without you. Also, Amy and her colleagues at White Magic studios who helped me to publish this book.

I apologise for the quality of the photographs that I took but hope they give a flavour of the interesting and beautiful places that I visited. I have endeavoured to be accurate in my reporting of information and road numbers etc but please forgive me if I have unwittingly made an error.

Thankyou for taking the time to read this book and I hope it encourages others to have their own adventure.

www.ingramcontent.com/pod-product-compliance
Lightning Source LLC
Chambersburg PA
CBHW041139110526
44590CB00027B/4076